# Bad Seeds
# and Holy Terrors

THE SUNY SERIES

HORIZONS of CINEMA

MURRAY POMERANCE | EDITOR

Also in the series

William Rothman, editor, *Cavell on Film*

J. David Slocum, editor, *Rebel Without a Cause*

Joe McElhaney, *The Death of Classical Cinema*

Kirsten Moana Thompson, *Apocalyptic Dread*

Frances Gateward, editor, *Seoul Searching*

Michael Atkinson, editor, *Exile Cinema*

Paul S. Moore, *Now Playing*

Robin L. Murray and Joseph K. Heumann, *Ecology and Popular Film*

William Rothman, editor, *Three Documentary Filmmakers*

Sean Griffin, editor, *Hetero*

Jean-Michel Frodon, editor, *Cinema and the Shoah*

Carolyn Jess-Cooke and Constantine Verevis, editors, *Second Takes*

Matthew Solomon, editor, *Fantastic Voyages of the Cinematic Imagination*

R. Barton Palmer and David Boyd, editors, *Hitchcock at the Source*

William Rothman, *Hitchcock, Second Edition*

Joanna Hearne, *Native Recognition*

Marc Raymond, *Hollywood's New Yorker*

Steven Rybin and Will Scheibel, editors, *Lonely Places, Dangerous Ground*

# Bad Seeds and Holy Terrors

## The Child Villains of Horror Film

Dominic Lennard

Cover image: Village of the Damned (John Carpenter, Alphaville, 1995). Photofest.

Published by State University of New York Press, Albany

For information, contact State University of New York Press, Albany, NY www.sunypress.edu

Production by Eileen Nizer
Marketing by Fran Keneston

**Library of Congress Cataloging-in-Publication Data**

Lennard, Dominic.
  Bad seeds and holy terrors : the child villains of horror film / Dominic Lennard.
      pages cm — (SUNY series, horizons of cinema)
  Includes bibliographical references and index.
  ISBN 978-1-4384-5329-3 (hc : alk. paper) 978-1-4384-5328-6 (pb : alk. paper)
  ISBN 978-1438-4-5330-9 (ebook)
  1. Horror films—History and criticism.   2. Children in motion pictures.
3. Villains in motion pictures.   I. Title.

PN1995.9.H6L385  2014
791.43'6164—dc23                                                    2013046285

10 9 8 7 6 5 4 3 2 1

*To Murray Pomerance*

# Contents

# Figures

# Acknowledgments

In producing this book, I relied on the support, wisdom, friendship, and patience of several people. From the University of Tasmania, I would like to thank especially my friends Michelle Phillipov, Craig Norris, and Rose Gaby for their conversation and collegial support. I am indebted to Elle Leane, who helped me to clarify aspects of this book in its own uncertain infancy, and also for the inspiration and guidance she has provided over the years. I am grateful for suggestions made by Joe Grixti (Massey University) on developing several foundational points in the introduction. I am also thankful for the advice of Simon Koop on the rise of child protection agencies, which assisted in my research into the public conceptualization of children in the early twentieth century. For their advice on developing the manuscript, I am also especially grateful to Linda Ruth Williams (University of Southampton) and Steven Woodward (Bishop's University). During much of the time spent completing this book, I have been thankful for the teaching opportunities provided by Lynn Jarvis and the support and friendship of my colleagues in the Centre for University Pathways and Partnerships at the University of Tasmania. To my students, past and present, many of whom have demonstrated such heartening interest in my work: your encouragement and interest means more to me than you know. I am enduringly grateful to Corinna Giblin for her wisdom, warm conversation, and patient reading of draft material. For their friendship, advice, conversation, and inspiration, I would also like to thank Imelda Whelehan, Adam Ouston, Samu Rahn, and Mikala Jayatilaka. I am also thankful to James Peltz at SUNY Press for his interest in my work and advice throughout its completion, and for the excellent work of Eileen Nizer and Laura Tendler Gallaher during the production and editing processes. To Murray Pomerance (Ryerson University), who has so often thrilled me with his wit and insight, moved me with his generosity, and whose conversations have been the most peculiar treat: my thanks are scarcely enough, but here they are. I would like to warmly acknowledge the support of my parents, Tony and Lee-Anne Lennard, and my brother and sister, Kristian and Anna. Finally, thanks to my faithful dog, Ahab, in tribute to his companionship, affection, and his very charming villainy.

An earlier version of the chapter "All Fun and Games till Someone Gets Hurt: Hating Children's Culture" appeared in volume 26, no. 3 of *Continuum: Journal of Media and Culture Studies* (2012) under the title "All Fun and Games . . . : Children's Culture in the Horror Film, from *Deep Red* (1975) to *Child's Play* (1988)."

# Little Horrors: Introduction

Despite their absence as viewers, children turn up a great deal in horror films. Steered diligently from the shadier shelves of video stores and libraries by watchful protectors, how could children know that they haunt iconic classics like *The Exorcist* (1973) and *The Omen* (1976) as well as marginal B pictures like *Beware! Children at Play* (1989) or *Whisper* (2007)? As mainstay villains of a type of film produced and consumed largely behind their backs, children are oblivious to the true weight and hyperbole of their representation on film, to the fantastical expressions of unease they inspire. With unquestioning zeal, adults reiterate and reinscribe their role as custodians of the child's proper knowledge, often with a resolution that sees childhood besieged by sex and violence everywhere. Children are unaware of what a burden they present because we are of a mind to plead ignorance ourselves—forever reconstructing a child to be, above all, protected. As in an obsessive ritual, we assure and reassure ourselves with visions of the innocent child: the little wonder, the beautiful victim, the cutie-pie rebel whose diminutive insurrections come more as flattery of our power than a challenge to it. Over the last sixty years, however, the horror film has played out the most stunning tantrums of mistrust. It has offered a unique domain where, with a nervous I-can't-help-but-look daring, adults raise the dust ruffle of the cinema curtain to discover the child they have always feared.

Some of these little horrors are zombies or other grotesques, as in George A. Romero's *Night of the Living Dead* (1968) or *The Exorcist*. Such portrayals court our adoration of, and sympathy for, the innocent child, only to shockingly betray it. In the innocent's place, we get the ingrate brute, the sacred terror, the evil-innocent; and our reverence for the immaculate child is never more powerful than when the one before us rudely decomposes.

Figure I.1. The innocent child's (Linda Blair's) deterioration in William Friedkin's *The Exorcist* (Warner Bros., 1973) fascinates and anguishes our ordinarily adoring gaze. Digital frame enlargement.

More often, child villains are insolently composed, as in *The Bad Seed* (1956) or *The Good Son* (1993). They head off our attempts to approach them as inferiors with intolerable pomp and are morphed into tricksters whose angelic appearance betrays their wanton manipulation of their adult audience. Some such children, as in *Village of the Damned* (1960), are all eyes, adepts of the accusatory look, braced by a self-disciplined silence. These are children who aggravate us with the smugly passive-aggressive suggestion that they might have something on us. So thoroughgoing, in fact, is the adult suspicion of the child played out by the horror film that it extends even to the demonization of the child's culture. Films like *Child's Play* (1988) and *Dolly Dearest* (1992), both of which center on possessed children's toys, illustrate the terror of childish imaginations unbounded by the prescriptions of adult authority.

Monstrousness, devilry, and dominion over a hostile alien culture have all been attributed to the child in the horror film as a flip side of the meanings Western culture imagines childhood to embody. This book examines the child villain, feverishly dreamt and redreamt in the horror film, as a side effect of the ideological colonization of childhood. It identifies the ways in which the meanings that are projected onto children, and which they seem to physically evidence, are inevitably exposed to horrifying and sensational contradiction. Through such contradictions, we can see the child's relationship to entrenched notions of class hierarchy, gender and parenting inequality, consumerism, and sexuality, all of which must be recognized as key discourses governing the relationship between adults and children historically and today.

This book focuses on fictional and often highly pejorative representations confined to an adult medium—that is, on cultural constructions. The definition of "child" that flows throughout does not observe any strict criteria based on age or physiological development. Rather, it fixes on dominant discourses of childhood, observing when these cultural constructions are being employed. For one example, the child as a construction and type with which we are familiar clearly punctuates the conclusion of Peter Brook's adaptation of *Lord of the Flies* (1963), when a naval officer wanders onto the island schoolboys have colonized, his figure captured in a slow tilt upward from the shoes that traces how toweringly "adult" he is. As the man casts his elevated gaze over the Eden the children have by now shockingly demolished, the child before him (and suddenly so small at his feet) bawls for the loss of a familiar childhood. The idea of the child can easily be deduced in cases like this, where there is a clear concern for the child *as* child, where diminutive people are referred to as "children"; in more general terms, the idea leans on our grasp of a film's unannounced (although very potent) attitude to its own representations. What the various incarnations of the child villain have in common is that they present children not doing what adults suppose they should be doing. They depict children behaving not only contrary to adult characters' wishes but also contrary to the behavior garden-variety "common sense" seems to designate appropriate for and natural to children.

In fact, a cornerstone of this book is the reconsideration of "common sense" conceptions of the child. When child-welfare advocates denounce the scourge of children's access to sexual information or violence with the sound-bite battle cry that children "should be allowed to be *children*," both the force and vagueness of ideological assumptions surrounding the child are pointedly apparent (indeed, such phrases deploy inscrutability itself as a political force). This project is about asking what, for the adult, "the child" means and, more to the point, why we are so disturbed when our definitions of children are contradicted.

No one has ever denied that a physiological childhood is universal, though many cultural theorists have focused on the manner in which societies understand this physical reality and confuse it with its ideological construction. As historian Philippe Ariès's work on the role of childhood in early modern Europe first informed us (even after its methodology was duly interrogated), childhood has by no means been fixed. Given the sheer ideological force of children's representation and interpretation, they are easily subject to fears generated by the expectations we have of them. The child villain can be seen to illustrate the otherwise unquestioned and powerfully felt meanings projected onto children—meanings cast into hideous relief by the trauma of their disruption. Equally significantly, in many of these films we can see an ideological reinforcement of the child-with-whom-we-are-adoringly-familiar through the sheer aberrance of its contradiction. That is, the child villain's anomalous evil ensures that he or she can only be ejected altogether from categories of childhood, leaving entrenched definitions of desirable children unquestioned (and thus prone to future upheaval).

The horror film is a compelling site for examining conflict and contradiction in the relationship between children and adults in Western culture for a number of reasons. In spite of the genre's lowbrow or unserious reputation, horror films are serious enough that we flinch at the idea of children being permitted to freely see them. Rick Worland writes:

> Most public discussions of fictional horror center around issues of censorship, the violation of social standards of morality and conduct, and the potentially deleterious results from exposure of some members of society, especially children and the socially disadvantaged, to violent, disturbing, and destabilizing horror narratives. (7)

The horror film's production, distribution, and consumption are based on an unspoken pretext that demands maturity of the audience as well as a spoken, legal pretext dictated by classification boards (according to which viewer sophistication and corruptibility are indexed by age) and by parents and adult guardians. Everything about horror films seems to mark them as specifically grown-up pleasures. Yet, as Worland points out, "[h]orror often achieves its greatest impact when it exposes or flaunts cultural taboos" (3). With this curious combination of a lowbrow status and the restriction to "mature" audiences, the horror film becomes an imaginary province where adults are temporarily granted license to behave or imagine themselves as children. It is common to hear devotion to horror films spoken of as a "childish" pleasure, an assertion that both indicates our disrespect for children and projects our own socially unacceptable impulses onto them. In enjoying horror's mess and tantrums, the adult pretends to be an innocent and in doing so takes up the behavior of the unpredictable child he or she seeks so scrupulously to shield. Children, meanwhile, must experience cinematic fantasies different from those of adults, which may encourage us to appreciate and depoliticize "a good scare." Horror is unquestioningly placed in opposition to the pedagogical/media sphere to which children are ideally confined, with its "innocent" (that is, ideologically sanctioned) genres and formats. Children must consume media quarantined from horror's tendency to "make fun" of open violence, stupidity, sadism, or sexuality: only adults get to act up this way and this much.

A self-consciously "adult" or "mature" approach to horror that acknowledges and dispenses with its extremity, knowingly embracing or dismissing its apparent "silliness," also belies the genre's serious side. Horror is an archetypal "lowbrow" form, after all, and thus a particularly interesting subject for the simple reason that common sense tells us it should not be scrutinized. As a genre, horror can use its perceived immunity to serious critique to get away with murder. This is one reason why its representations have been the subject of considerable academic interest. William Paul writes that "the negative definition of the lower works would have it that they are less subtle than higher genres. More positively, it could be said that they are more direct" (32). Given the ironically oppositional relationship horror viewing shares with childhood, it is not at all surprising that the genre has served as a depository of adult ambivalence toward children. Among the most significant of these films are *The Bad Seed, Village of the Damned, Rosemary's Baby* (1968), *The Exorcist, It's Alive* (1974), *The Omen, The Brood* (1979), *The Ring* (2002), and *Orphan* (2009), as well as a wealth of lesser-known pictures such as *Kill Baby, Kill* (1966), *The Other* (1972), *It's Alive 2: It Lives Again* (1978), *Phenomena* (1985), *It's Alive III: Island of the Alive* (1987), *The Suckling* (1990), *The Good Son, 666: The Demon Child* (2004), *Godsend* (2004), *The Omen* (2006), *666: The Child* (2006), *Zombies* (aka *Wicked Little Things*) (2006), *The Plague* (2006), *Whisper* (2007), *Joshua* (aka *Joshua: The Devil's Child*, 2007), *Home Movie* (2008), and *The Awakening* (2011).

Child villains propagated by horror have proven so striking that they have not only been formalized into clichés within horror but extended into other genres and formats. In *The X Files* (1993–2002) episode "Chinga," the spoiled, sulky-faced daughter of a single mother uses her toy doll to hypnotize those who irritate her into enacting a creative array of suicides. These hypno-suicides strongly recall *Village of the Damned*, while the focus on a cursed doll recalls the anxieties surrounding children's culture that undergird films like *Child's Play* (1988), *Dolly Dearest*, and *Demonic Toys* (1992). The comically Machiavellian baby of the cartoon series *Family Guy* (1999–) owes much to the overdemanding and sophisticated children of horror film (the allusion is completed with reference to *The Omen* in one episode ["Death is a Bitch"]). Harry Potter's bratty nemesis, Draco Malfoy (Tom Felton), revitalizes the figure of the obnoxiously upper-class child villain recognizable from *The Bad Seed* and *The Omen*, a figure who delights in making his wealth and status oppressively clear. Similarly, although with more startling malice, the blond-haired and proudly blue-blooded child king, Joffrey Baratheon (Jack Gleeson), of HBO's *Game of Thrones* (2011–), upon ascending illegitimately to the throne, enacts his effete bloodlust with impunity. AMC's hit zombie series *The Walking Dead* (2010–) punctuates its opening scene with the transformation of the child into one of the hideous undead—the same transformation at the center of Romero's *Night of the Living Dead*. Here, the set of bunny slippers we see shuffling along the pavement is inhabited not, as one might expect, by an abandoned darling in need of rescue by the sheriff's deputy protagonist, but by its monstrous inverse: a groaning, blood-besmeared and smashed-faced atrocity requiring the swiftest euthanasia law enforcement's six-shooters can deliver. In Lynne Ramsay's *We Need to Talk About Kevin* (2011), the child psychopath of films like *The Bad Seed*, *The Good Son*, and *Orphan* is legitimized through the "serious" experimental stylings of art-house cinema. John Moore's 2006 remake of *The Omen* demonstrates the child villain's continuing hold on the popular imagination, as do newer additions to the juvenile lineup, including the frighteningly empowered children of *Hard Candy* (2006) and *Orphan* (2009). Both of these films reconstruct the child villain in response to recognizably new anxieties surrounding children in Western culture.

## To Catch Them Unawares: Horror's Evil Innocents

In light of children's absence as creative producers of popular film (and the intricacy of their management as performers), we have particular license to question their representations within it, especially given the cultural dominance of their association with innocence. In 1982, Neil Postman, noting what he saw as television's refusal to distinguish between child and adult viewers, pessimistically forecasted childhood's erasure as a cultural category in his book *The Disappearance of Childhood*. Postman's exaggerations are apparent at various points. For instance, as evidence of childhood's disappearance, he suggests that "Hide-and-Seek . . . has almost completely disappeared from the repertoire of self-organized children's amusements" (4). (This is news to me; I grew up entirely in the period after Postman's book was published and played the game frequently as a child.) Postman also confidently announces that "children have virtually disappeared from the media, especially from television" (122); even with his caveat (he means children who aren't simply depicted as small adults), such a claim seems more symptomatic of cultural interest in policing the boundaries between children and adults than a diagnostic assertion. In retrospect, we can see that the conceptualization of children has remained surprisingly consistent. Allison James and Chris Jenks point out that

> Notwithstanding differences in accounts of childhood's pure state, nor yet of the purpose and intent of its usage, over time, the theme of innocence has remained closely tied to "the child." It would be hard to envisage any other group in modern society content to be suspended within such essentially anachronistic visions. Nevertheless they persist. (320)

Past critical studies of fictional children have overwhelmingly acknowledged the endurance of Romantic notions of childhood, in which these visions of innocence were first entrenched (see, for example, Kuhn; Pattison; and Merlock Jackson). The erosion of confidence in rationalist philosophy that characterized the aftermath of the Revolutionary era, and the conflict between the artist and the society in which he or she lived, had lasting effects on artistic representations to come. In *The Image of Childhood*, Peter Coveney provides an extensive early investigation into the image of the child in literature. As he points out, whereas prior to the late eighteenth century the child was an absent, insignificant, or narrowly allegorical figure,

> [in] a world given increasingly to utilitarian values and the Machine, the child could become the symbol of Imagination and Sensibility, a symbol of Nature set against the forces abroad in society actively de-naturing humanity. Through the child the artist could express his awareness of the conflict between human Innocence and the cumulative pressures of social Experience. (31)

It is through these ideas that the mythologization of childhood began to be established as an enduring aspect of the Western cultural and artistic legacy.

This transformation of thought on childhood is heavily indebted to Jean-Jacques Rousseau, whose immensely influential treatise on education, *Émile* (1762), decisively asserted that nothing "natural" could be a priori sinful and outlined childhood as an emotional and intellectual state to be nurtured rather than educated out.[1] For Rousseau and the representative tradition he helped to inspire, the "natural" child was always and immediately innocent, and the rigors of preemptive education and socialization threatened to distort his or her unique and wondrous nature. Hugh Cunningham perhaps best summarizes the Romantic ide-ology of the child:

> At its heart was a reverence for, and a sanctification of child-hood which was at total odds with the Puritan emphasis on the child as a sinful being. Romanticism embedded in the European and American mind a sense of the importance of childhood, a belief that childhood should be happy, and a hope that the qualities of childhood, if they could be preserved in adult-hood, might help redeem the adult world. (Cunningham 72)

The conceptualization of the child as an innocent to be sheltered and morally guided and a figure in whom adults tenderly invested their hopes for the future was recharged during the first decades of the twentieth century. Children's employment lost its earlier vital significance to the family economy as the rigors of child labor were placed under increasing legislative scrutiny and as infant mortality declined in both prevalence and cultural tolerability. Viviana Zelizer suggests that from the 1870s to the 1930s, the "twentieth-century economically useless but emotionally priceless [child] displaced the nineteenth-century useful child. . . . The new sacred child occupied a special and separate world, regulated by affection and education, not work or profit" (209). The resentimental-ization of childhood was aided by the "child-saving" movement, which channeled the feminist desire for increased participation in civic life into traditionally feminine roles of motherhood and nurturing.[2]

Cinema followed prevailing tradition in perpetuating notions of children's fundamental innocence and vulnerability. Kathy Merlock Jack-son astutely observes that at the same time that the needs and particular psychology of real children were under increasing scrutiny, "the turn of the twentieth century saw the imagined innocence of childhood being idealized as never before in Western culture" (27). The differing images of the Romantic child that have prevailed in Western film and literature over the past three centuries have in common that they foreground the child's fundamental innocence and, implicitly or explicitly, his or her need of protection—and, thus, his or her subordination. Even in those films where the child is somehow (usually supernaturally rather than socially) empow-ered, such as in *The Shining* (1980) or *Firestarter* (1984), the assumption of fragility and need for (adult) protection is heavily underscored.

Children have traditionally and with considerable ubiquity been used as an embodiment of innocence, and, following this, they are also frequently positioned to thoroughly besmirch in the viewer's eyes those who would harm them. The murder of the child is familiar to the cinemagoer as the mark of an irredeemable barbarism—for they are all of them innocents, these child victims. A shot and trampled child, then a runaway baby carriage, form the climax of the celebrated Odessa Steps sequence in Eisenstein's *Battleship Potemkin* (1925), cementing, above all, the inhumanity of the Tsarist soldiers. In Fritz Lang's *M* (1931) the serial murder of children is so intolerable that, with efficiency and vehemence rivaling that of the police, even the criminal underworld begins hunting the man responsible. As a barmaid explains, not only does the police search disrupt criminal business and offensively associate workaday hoods with a reprobate child murderer, but "everyone is a little mother at heart. I know a lot of crooks who get sort of tender when they see kids." At the beginning of Leone's *Once Upon A Time In The West* (1968), the callous murder of the stoic Irish child by hired gun Frank (Henry Fonda)[3] forms the climax of the massacre of the whole family: frozen before a phalanx of gunmen, the boy obediently clutches a carafe of wine like an altar boy—a moment clearly wrapped up in what Zelizer has referred to as the sacralization of childhood (see *Pricing the Priceless Child*). The film here confirms the suppression of Puritan notions of Original Sin in favor of an intersection of Romantic and Catholic ideas that position children closer to God. The bandit Cheyenne (Jason Robards) bolsters this sacralizing notion later when he is accused of the crime himself: "I'll kill anything . . . Never a kid: like killing a priest. Catholic priest, that is." In the opening of another Western, Sam Peckinpah's *The Wild Bunch* (1969), two children, caught in the middle of the mother of all shootouts, brace each other as horses crash and rifles roar around them. As numerous commentators have pointed out, the violence depicted here is horrifyingly random: all manner of pedestrians are caught in the cross fire, felled in perversely balletic slow motion or thundered over by crazed horses. Yet the endangered children are held in nervous reserve as that violence's worst-case scenario, our urgent concern for their survival sustaining the scene's tension. Moreover, the violence of the scene is amplified through crosscutting that constantly shows us the children's faces; while those tiny faces are clenched against a veritable hurricane of dust, they nevertheless follow the chaos around which it swirls. The scene seems more violent not only because children are stuck in the middle of it but also because they witness its every horrific detail. And in James Cameron's blockbuster *Titanic* (1997), as the ship sinks lower into the sea, Cal Hockley (Billy Zane), obnoxious steel heir and jilted fiancé of heroine Rose DeWitt Bukater (Kate Winslet), snatches up a crying girl, artfully performing as her "father" in a ploy to secure himself a place on a lifeboat. Hockley disgracefully mimics parental care for one who, alone the middle of the most iconic disaster of the twentieth century, is

vulnerability personified. The effortless cunning of his design, his successful yet empty performance of emotional connection, and most of all
the *object* of his exploitation amass to confirm for the viewer the depth
of his despicability.

If we cannot precisely call the innocent child a stock character given
that to do so would overstate the homogeneity of children's representation, we can at least say that children's innocence and vulnerability is
routinely and unquestioningly referenced, posited as assumed cultural
knowledge that requires no special development within the diegesis itself.
Even when we know utterly nothing about the child we are watching
(as in all of these examples and innumerable others), we already have a
strong idea of how we're expected to feel about her. To a very real yet
unexamined extent, we already know what the child *means*.

In the horror film, the regular use of the child as a victim sustains
and even amplifies this characterization. The bedridden daughter of *The
Sixth Sense* (1999) indicates the vileness of the mother who has been
poisoning her all along. The creepy diabolism of slasher icon Freddy
Krueger of *Nightmare on Elm Street* (1984) is ensured by his status as a
child murderer. Just as the child's powerlessness is always evoked before
it he or she is attacked, the child is always innocent before he or she is
villainous. In Romero's *Night of the Living Dead*, the child's motionless
body is positioned as the subject of intense sympathy for the majority
of the film, "an image of absolute dependency," in the words of William
Paul, "someone who must be constantly cared for and fretted over by
her distraught parents" (261), before the girl finally comes to life and
hacks her mother to death with a trowel (in the moment that prefigures
*The Walking Dead*). When two silent, jumpsuited children approach an
amiable young kindergarten teacher in *The Brood*, then bludgeon her to
death with toy hammers in the middle of a classroom, it is clear that the
scene's horror owes something to the precursory imitation of a familiar
figure: the child-as-potential-victim, the endearing, innocent tot requiring guidance and care. Cinema's evil child we don't expect is one whose
cunning, sadism, or menace implicitly references the child we *do*, the
child we believe in. Freud describes feelings of uncanniness as stemming
from a similar mismatch of expectations. In order to feel this species of
dread, we have to feel certain of the reality that is under threat—thus,
we are presented with *two* realities intolerably vying for priority. The
uncanny, he writes, "cannot arise unless there is, for the receiver of the
text, an implicit conflict of judgment as to the validity of its proposi-
tions" (250). Similarly, the effect of the child villain is dependent on his
or her confronting betrayal of a familiar "real" child. There is nothing
up front about the child's villainy; Merlock Jackson is certainly on the

money when she writes that what portrayals of child villains suggest "is conflict, not abiding acceptance" (152): these are representations founded on our very inability and unwillingness to accept them, the investment in the child as vulnerable and innocent ensuring that contrary depictions manifest as paranoiac visions of tyranny and evil.

This dynamic, in its challenge to an anachronistic vision of innocence—the reality of which we can never quite be certain—bears some resemblance to what Robin Wood described as the "return of the repressed" in his seminal 1979 essay "An Introduction to the American Horror Film." Horror's tendency is to confront us with what (bourgeois capitalist) society must repress so that it can maintain its current form and with what we must personally repress in order to become accepted citizens. Outlining subjects of anxiety in the contemporary horror film, Wood draws attention to the child as Other, although he approaches the issue from a somewhat different perspective. For Wood, children are Othered in horror because they are a reminder of "childish" impulses that we must energetically repress to become socially validated members of society: they evoke for us a stage in which the infantile urges and complexes discussed by Freud remained troublingly unresolved (113).

This perspective, part of psychoanalysis's historical dominance of critical inquiry into horror, has intriguing limitations. For all the advances of psychoanalysis in dismantling the mythic innocence of the child, critics such as Joseph Zornado and Maria Tatar have pointed out that the legacy of Freud also had the ironic effect of stunting further investigation into the relationship between children and adults by casting the child as inherently volatile. Through the Oedipus complex, the image of the child that Freudian theory develops is of an uncontrolled, even murderous bundle of impulses that must eventually submit to the restrictions of (adult) society (see Zornado 39). Thus, the revelations of Freudian theory had a hand in the further obfuscation of the socially structured relationship between children and adults and the validation of a Victorian child-rearing status quo as inevitable. The interpretation of the child as representative of uncontrolled urges tends to construct a biologically "factual" child, omitting the significance of children's social conceptualization, of how we perceive them. Wood's notion of a "return of the repressed" becomes more pertinent, however, in a broader sense through Western culture's strenuous disacknowledgment of children's agency or right to it. When children are the primary investment of any status quo, their subordination and vulnerability to the dominant order is of great significance. However, as this book demonstrates, the child villain always possesses a degree of shocking autonomy that fantastically illustrates the agency and power that children are denied in our society.

More useful in circumscribing the nature and effect of child villainy, especially in relation to the apparently innocent and powerless child, is the work of Noël Carroll, with its emphasis on conflicting cultural categories. For Carroll, our response to the monster at the center of the horror film is consistent with confronting a kind of impurity. In explaining this response, he draws on the anthropological work of Mary Douglas, who relates reactions of impurity to perceived transgressions of accepted cultural categories. Cultural order involves a reliance on familiar classifications, and the horror monster's category violations, its confusions and border-crossings, upset our conceptual schema:

> Many monsters of the horror genre are interstitial and/or con-tradictory in terms of being both living and dead: ghosts, zom-bies, vampires, mummies. . . . Also many monsters confound different species: werewolves, humanoid insects, humanoid reptiles, and the inhabitants of Dr. Moreau's island. . . . The creature in Howard Hawks's classic *The Thing* is an intelligent, twolegged, bloodsucking carrot. Now that's interstitial. (32)

Horror monsters "are un-natural relative to a culture's conceptual scheme of nature. They do not fit the scheme; they violate it. Thus, monsters are not only physically threatening; they are cognitively threatening" (34). Conceptualizations of the child as innocent circulate so power-fully and without critique as to be rendered "natural." Consequently, the child's contradiction of the powerless image ascribed to him or her, such a demolition of the hierarchy between adult and child, attaches to this child the kind of horrific cognitive dissonance outlined by Carroll. It is the child villain's intolerable confusion of cultural categories that renders him or her so potent, a confusion only increased through the sentimentality invested in apparently "natural" definitions of childhood.

However, children in cinema represent more than just innocence, signifying for us a plurality of complex roles elicited and exploited by dif-ferent constructions of the child villain, roles that the concept of "inno-cence" frequently works to abstract and disguise. Drawing on a variety of critical discourses including children's cultural studies, Marxism, psycho-analysis, and film theory, this book inspects the immense baggage of the child's symbolic meaning and interrogates the preconceptions on which villainous children press down uncomfortably. Where the child villain occurs in the horror film, so do any number of corresponding cultural impressions through which he or she is defined. In this way, a major objective of this study is the exploration of what it is that the child villain is relative *to*—the discovery of what we presume about the "real" child.

Analysis of the child villain in horror, I maintain, unveils the powerful symbolism of the culturally constructed child. It exposes our deepseated reliance on understanding both ourselves and our society through children, and the volatility of the assumptions we make. We may have been frightening ourselves for years with the child villain, dragging him or her out like a crude parlor game when the real children have gone to bed, but we have not seriously believed in the inherent evilness of the child. The child villain speaks to conflicts in every sense unacknowledged and indicates the stubbornness of the adult conception of childhood as an apolitical site of nostalgia. As Zornado argues, "The adult's conscious desire to dismiss childhood as a time of innocence and insubstantiality when attempting to understand adult life is an enactment of the dominant ideology, and therefore a significant ideological moment in the production and reproduction of the dominant culture" (215). Uncertainties surrounding that construct can only take us by surprise because we simply refuse to acknowledge the ideological character of our definitions of childhood, to stop confusing them with the real child. As long as we insist on anticipating incontrovertible innocence, the child villain always emerges from a place of the unknown, capitalizing on the very force of our denial.

## The Plot

In light of the 1956 release of archetypal evil-child film *The Bad Seed* (responsible for introducing the term "bad seed" to popular culture as a label for one "born bad"), a number of writers on children in film have identified the evil child's genesis in the 1950s (e.g., Paul; Merlock Jackson; Creed; Kincheloe; Petley), albeit while offering minimal or no account of why. In my first chapter, I seek to explain the sensational emergence of the child villain through this era's uneasy reassessment of childhood innocence. This reassessment played out through panic over juvenile delinquency, treated cinematically in films like *The Wild One* (1953), *Blackboard Jungle* (1955), and *Rebel Without a Cause* (1955). Following discussion and contextualization of these films, I trace the path of this questioning of childhood into horror film through *The Bad Seed*, which provided the preconditions for the child to be formulated as a monster in the tradition of the genre. So influential was this film, in which an outwardly perfect child is in fact a ruthless killer, that the reader will find that discussion of it recurs at various points throughout this book in several different though equally important contexts.

In my second chapter, I begin to investigate more closely some of the crucial, if unacknowledged, discourses that surround childhood through their dramatic disruption by the child villain, observing that the child villain in films like *The Bad Seed*, *Village of the Damned*, and *The Omen* is a curiously class-specific figure. Regarding the proliferation of evil children in 1970s horror (e.g., *The Exorcist*, *It's Alive*, *The Omen*, *Holocaust 2000* [1977]), Merlock Jackson suggests that, by this decade, "as Americans faced soaring inflation and a rising cost of living, they saw children as a greater financial burden" (147). Yet this supposition is challenged by the consistency with which terrible children are identifiable as upper-class figures born of wealthy, financially successful parents, and challenged further when one considers the child stars of the 1930s, an era when audiences for whom having children was a financial burden delighted in seeing them onscreen. As it happens, what I call the "bourgeois brat" provides perhaps the most recognizable incarnation of the child villain in horror, inaugurated with films like *The Bad Seed* and *Village of the Damned*, and repeated in innumerable pictures since, from *The Omen* and *Resident Evil* (2002) to hammy B-grade productions like *Demonic Toys*. With special reference to two films, *The Bad Seed* and *Village of the Damned*, I discuss the evil child's relationship to socioeconomic dominance and his or her tendency to make ideological violence horrifyingly literal.

In my third chapter, I turn my attention to one of the child villain's most recognizable and characteristic behaviors: maintaining a stare of utter mute refusal toward whomever opposes him or her. The eyes of the children in *Village of the Damned* (as in John Wyndham's novel, *The Midwich Cuckoos*, from which it was adapted) glow with supernatural menace as their hypnotized victims are telepathically instructed to self-harm. The image of a child threatening clear physical violence might be an untenable or even ridiculous one. But what they can do—to significant effect—is *look*. In many films featuring evil children, the child's stare is either unsettlingly lingered upon or capable of causing injury outright. I take the gaze as a motif that expresses child/adult separation and disrupts conceptualizations of childhood enforced by the way children are ordinarily looked at. With particular reference to *Village of the Damned* (1960 and 1995) and the famous opening scene of John Carpenter's *Halloween* (1978), I argue that the assignment of meaning to children is profoundly dependent on the act of spectatorship and the presumption that adult control will be consolidated through it.

As far back as *The Bad Seed*, which Paul suggests "makes clear an anxiety about female power" through the characterization of a mother who is "necessarily incapable of dealing with something that requires more potent action" (280–81), films featuring child villains have been distinguished by their morally inept or monstrous mother figures. The irrational woman who fosters and defends an evil child is a consistent presence in these films (further examples include *Phenomena* and *Kill Baby, Kill*), and my fourth chapter discusses the relationship between the mother and the evil child. Horror film criticism has long dwelled on the "monstrous-feminine" theorized by Barbara Creed, in which female reproductive power is demonized. I discuss the implication of this idea for the child's representation, demonstrating in David Cronenberg's *The Brood* a deep distrust of maternal devotion to children as well as uncertainty grounded in women's transforming social roles. However, this chapter also proceeds to a discussion of Roman Polanski's *Rosemary's Baby*, in which a mother incubates the child of a satanic cult, a premise in which we can perceive a grim and conspiratorial metaphor for the stifling containment of women during maternity.

Women's social roles were again centralized in the child villain's resurgence through Gore Verbinski's *The Ring* (2002), although reformulated to suit modern anxieties. In my fifth chapter, through in-depth discussion of this film, I discuss the child villain's relationship to changing discourses of parenting and child autonomy in late modernity as well as note a resurrection of anxieties over children's familiarity with mass media.

My approach to children in horror places unique emphasis on the socially determined structure of paternity (a greatly overlooked theme of modern horror), and in my sixth chapter I analyze *The Omen* (one of the most renowned of evil-child films), particularly its challenge to the nature of fatherhood, before moving on to explore the child's role in sustaining and naturalizing dominant ideology. In the second part of this chapter, I turn my attention to Larry Cohen's *It's Alive* in order to consider how the dominance of patriarchal views of reproduction mean that the birth of a monstrous child is constructed as a slur on his father's masculinity.

Chapter 7 returns to one of cinema's most iconic visions of child villainy, exploring the spectacularly marred innocence of the possessed Regan (Linda Blair) in *The Exorcist*. In discussing this film, I draw upon psychoanalytic ideas of selfhood that outline the power of one's *first* sense of self: the wonderful, magical child of the parent's gaze. I also direct attention to the priest, Damien Karras (Jason Miller), who comes to Regan's aid—a man whose mother has harrowingly renounced her son prior to her death, thus casting him in irrevocable opposition to his idealized self-image as the good child. Following this, I suggest that Regan's possession can be read as an illustration of the haunting power of internalized notions of childhood "purity" and "innocence."

In adult-audience genres, childishness is often cast as perverse delinquency. One need think only of the femme fatale Carmen (Martha Vickers) of *The Big Sleep* (1946), who conceals her cruelty behind airheadedness and juvenile coquetry, or the emotionally stunted Norman Bates of *Psycho* (1960). In the horror film, children's culture itself is frequently represented as a sinister and liminal aesthetic, a cutesy façade for the concealment of delirium or violence. In my eighth chapter, I address the horror film's treatment of children's culture particularly, discussing the popular horror film *Child's Play*, in which a hi-tech children's doll is possessed by the spirit of a murderer, in connection with a rise in marketing to children during the 1980s. I argue that the film's demonic image of children's culture can be traced to the financial pressure placed on parents to purchase the latest consumer products, presenting children's emotional longings as a threat to adult power.

The often feverish social concern over pedophilia has also affected the representation of child villains in horror, and in my final chapter I focus on two more recent films that engaged with this theme in intriguing, related, yet differing ways. First, in *Hard Candy* (2005), a suspected pedophile gets more than he bargained for when he is drugged, tied, and tortured by the fourteen-year-old girl he attempts to seduce. Secondly, in *Orphan*, a couple's adopted daughter pursues the sexual attention of her new father. In contrast with earlier films, such *The Bad Seed*, *Village of the Damned*, and *The Omen*, *Hard Candy* gives us a child antagonist with whom we are encouraged to sympathize, even while she exacts her morally dubious "justice." I interrogate the way the film exploits the contemporary specter of pedophilia and our fear of being identified with it, pushing to the limit our devotion to the innocent and asexual child. The pedophilia theme gives us a child villain with whom we feel we have no choice but to go along. Similarly, *Orphan* reframes the child villain according to an obsessive cultural concern with keeping pedophilia at a distance.

The images of children presented to us by popular film hold immense political significance because of their ability to influence and reflect public perceptions. I intend this book as a very modest contribution to the project of reenvisioning the child in popular culture. Of course, by this I do not mean this book is about pinpointing a "real" child, nor is it about recreating children as "vacant subjects." Maria Tatar has criticized prominent literary and cultural theorist James R. Kincaid for constructing an "imaginative" interpretation of children's experiences—a narrative that "once again, projects feelings onto the constructed child without ever conferring with the real child" (742). Rather, this book is about reaching a new and overdue appreciation of the pervasiveness of children's ideological occupation by adults—about what we push on children and what they reflect for us. Attempting to understand real children (their personalities, passions, experiences, anxieties, and aggressions) through the horror film, a cultural medium from which they are formally excluded, would be fanciful. Rather, I am interested in how children are deciphered and interpreted by adults and in calling into question those decipherings and interpretations. The chapter, for instance, in which I analyze the child villain's unwavering gaze as a symbolic threat to adult power has nothing whatever to do with children's real desires or any real and practiced form of children's resistance to adult power. It has everything, however, to do with adult fear and, specifically, the adult investment in having the way they look at children confirm their own power over them. Similarly, my chapter on children's culture in the horror film details a nightmare vision of children's consumer desires, one irrelevant to the actual attachments, intensity, or psychology of those desires—but acutely relevant to their cultural perception by adults.

Of particular concern to me is the *continued* existence of the child villain as a type, in roles that, because we fail to recognize or reconsider them, are doomed to be repeated. However monstrous, psychopathic, malicious, or manipulative—however implausible—the child villain thrives in film precisely because he or she is "uncontroversial." Unlike, for instance, the sly Indians of early Westerns, horror's characterizations of children are still considered neither offensive nor political. The failure to recognize the images of children as derogatory reflections on our relationship with them, their social standing, and their subjecthood is an issue this book is directed toward exposing.

## It's Only a Movie

Not only have the child villains of horror stamped their influence on representations of wayward children in other genres, but, more worryingly, they have formed potent and surprisingly unironic points of reference in considerations of the nature of childhood in journalism and public discourse. It is difficult to determine to what degree our conceptualization of the child may have been arrested by the impersonations the horror film has put forward over the last fifty to sixty years. Salman Rushdie, in his 2001 article on the impending release of Robert Thompson and Jon Venables, who at the age of ten murdered toddler James Bulger in 1993, remarked that the "profound question" on the nature of evil raised by the two young murderers had been

> inevitably rendered shallow by the media, for whom evil appeared to be some sort of video nasty manifestation of the "demon seed" variety. It was indeed suggested that [the killers] had been influenced by a video nasty which, as it

turned out, they hadn't seen. But it wasn't the killers who thought in the clichéd stereotypes of horror fiction. It was the British press. (381)

Julian Petley has pointed out that Venables and Thompson were treated with a "demonic" vocabulary explicitly grounded in the horror film: "The *Telegraph* . . . alleged that Thompson's nickname was Damien [from *The Omen*] and, furthermore, that he was born on Friday the 13th" (105; see also David Green's "Suitable Vehicles: Framing Blame and Justice When Children Kill a Child"). In 2010, Eric Smith, incarcerated for sixteen years for murdering his four-year-old neighbor when he was thirteen, spoke out against his categorization according to these familiar stereotypes: "You can label me a monster, a cold-blooded killer, a demon child, Satan incarnate . . . I don't care what name you give me—it doesn't mean that's who I am" ("Teen killer speaks out 16 years later," *WIVB. com*). While innocent images of children may continue to prevail in film, it is undeniable that their worrisome doppelgängers are becoming more and more a part of the Western cultural imagination. That we may be willing to believe in the monstrousness circulated by the horror film marks an unambiguous descent, an avenue through which the real complexity of children and our relationships and responsibilities to them can be comfortably dismissed. The employment of the vocabulary of monstrosity marks a transition into what Joe Kincheloe refers to as "child-based xenophobia" (164). The moment we can identify the child as one of "those children," we can, at least in some sense, rest easy: his or her nature was inevitable. We can find easy pardon by saying to ourselves, and saying to the child, that *we tried*. What's more: we can say it in a voice we know full well is unanswerable.

# 1

# Reaching the Age of Anxiety

## The 1950s and the Horror of Youth

THREATS TO THE IDEA OF THE innocent and vulnerable child were perceived and denounced at various points in the first half of the twentieth century. However, in the years following World War II childhood became increasingly visible as a distinct and potentially troubling category. Youth culture was permitted to flourish after the Great Depression disconnected young people from their traditional economic roles, and enrollment in high school became normalized. The popularization of automobiles also gave teenagers increased mobility and freedom to congregate outside of a supervisory adult gaze. Concerns were raised particularly in light of an unprecedented national concern over youth crime. The actual increase of juvenile crime in the years following the war is uncertain (see James Gilbert's *A Cycle of Outrage* for detailed discussion of its uncertainties), but the public was easily drawn into the narrative of a dramatic increase with a number of cultural culprits. Centralized in the panic over wayward youth were the spread of mass media, namely television, an increasingly distinct youth culture (including rock and roll), and the popularity of comic books. Senator Estes Kefauver's 1955–56 report on comic books and juvenile delinquency (which preceded a similar inquiry into television) nervously observed the new ubiquity of the mass media:

The child today in the process of growing up is constantly
exposed to sights and sounds of a kind and quality undreamed
of in previous generations. As these sights and sounds can
be a powerful force for good, so too can they be a powerful
counterpoise working evil. Their very quantity makes them
a factor to be reckoned with in determining the total climate
encountered by today's children during their formative years.
("Comic Books and Juvenile Delinquency")

Providing expert testimony on the relationship between comic books and
juvenile crime before Kefauver's Senate Subcommittee on Juvenile Delinquency was Dr. Fredric Wertham, author of *Seduction of the Innocent*, an
excoriating explanation of the effect of comics on the educational, social,
criminal, and sexual trajectories of their young readers. In reference to
the popular crime comics of the era, Wertham wrote that while "almost
all good children's reading has some educational value, crime comics
by their very nature are anti-educational. They fail to teach anything
that might be useful to a child; they do suggest many things that are
harmful" (90). For Wertham, censorship of comics was urgently needed
for children's mental and social health and thus the health of society as
a whole. For example, Wertham outlined what he called the *comic-book
syndrome*, which occurs "in all children in all walks of life who are in
no way psychologically predisposed" (114). The "syndrome" provided a
direct narrative in which the process of reading and acquiring comics
led to juvenile delinquency: the comic books' antisocial subject matter aroused in the child antisocial impulses for which he or she felt
guilty—consequently, as Wertham saw it, further comics were obtained
clandestinely through dishonesty or theft.

Having infiltrated all the way into the "safe" domestic sphere, television was considered a threat through the sexual or violent content of
its programs as well as through its ability to address children directly,
bypassing the adult as caretaker of children's "appropriate" knowledge.
While the new medium was seen as a potentially useful domestic tool
through its ability to promote family values, moral panic over its uncertainties achieved a powerful foothold in the cultural imagination. Joe
Kincheloe observes that

[t]he popular press circulated stories about a six-year-old who
asked his father for real bullets because his sister didn't die
when he shot her with his toy gun, a seven-year-old who put
ground glass in the family's lamb stew, a nine-year-old who
proposed killing his teacher with a box of poison chocolates,

an eleven-year-old who shot his television set with his B. B. gun, a thirteen-year-old who stabbed her mother with a kitchen knife, and a sixteen-year-old who strangled a sleeping child to death—all, of course, after witnessing similar murders on television. (117)

Following (and in many cases contributing to) the public concern with delinquency, cinematic representations of youth changed dramatically, providing for children's passage into horror cinema as villains. Not that the horrifying child was entirely new; it is certainly true that prototypes of horror's child villain predate this era. In William Blake's poem "The Mental Traveller," the narrator conveys an immense but elusive dread at the spectacle of a frowning baby who parallels the infant Jesus. In Henry James's *The Turn of the Screw*, a well-meaning governess struggles with the veiled truth of her ward's delinquency, a trait strikingly posed against his idealized appearance. Similarly, it would be a mistake to view pre–World War II cinematic representations of children as entirely one-note in their affirmation of innocence; as Timothy Shary points out, "[t]he very association of children with innocence had been challenged throughout many films of the 1930s and 1940s, especially as studios developed films about social problems during the Depression" (15). However, it was in the 1950s that the cinematic questioning of childhood innocence attained new force with a plethora of films of greater and lesser repute focusing on juvenile delinquency. It was in this period, and via these concerns, that child villainy achieved the currency and force that allowed it to solidify into an enduring horror theme. The year 1956 saw the release of the archetypal child villain film, *The Bad Seed*. While it clearly drew on the moral panic juvenile delinquency sparked, *The Bad Seed* also strikingly decontextualized the deviance it depicted, shifting the discourse that surrounded the troubled child: a social problem interwoven with complex cultural developments became a problem of inherent evil. This chapter traces horror's child villains to the cycle of juvenile delinquent films of the 1950s, highlighting the cultural changes of the time that rocked categories of childhood. It also identifies *The Bad Seed* as a watershed film that transferred cinematic questioning of innocence from social commentary to horror, directing representations of transgressive children into new and more volatile forms.

## Troubled Teens: The Juvenile Delinquent on Film

As Shary points out, "There was no moment when the [juvenile delinquent] fixation of the 1950s begins in earnest. Certainly movies like *Knock on Any Door* were harbingers, yet not many delinquency tales were made before the mid-1950s" (50). Yet by the decade's close, a multitude of pictures of greater and lesser quality had been produced. Most influential and noteworthy in the cycle were certainly *The Wild One* (1953), *Blackboard Jungle* (1955), and *Rebel Without a Cause* (1955). In *The Wild One*, the delinquent was portrayed with fundamental sympathy, his rebellious appeal and redemptive possibilities combined in the leader of the Black Rebels Motorcycle Club, Johnny Strabler (Marlon Brando in possibly his most iconic role, and in a performance of standoffish naturalism that sent waves of influence through the world of young male actors). Upon arriving with his goons in the town that will be subject to their mayhem, and despite his status as leader to whom club members consistently defer, Johnny swiftly and sulkily distances himself from his gang, taking refuge in the local tavern. He carries through the film like a fetish a trophy stolen from a motorcycle race, a token of his disaffection; Johnny claims to be the legitimate owner of the prize yet makes no attempt to conceal its stolen origin, flaunting it as a genuine token of his social worth as well as an obnoxious parody of his desire for acceptance. In *The Wild One*, we can see a number of changes to youth's conceptualization that are characteristic of the era. Aggressively foregrounded is the visibility of a youth subculture (in the form of motorcycle gangs) as well as a young man's ambivalent desire to be accepted by an increasingly self-absorbed adult culture, a self-absorption elaborated most memorably in *Rebel Without a Cause* (1955). More than mere anxiety over an increasingly autonomous youth culture, the gang's thunderous arrival—swarming into the town like black leather hornets—also gestures to the mobility granted by a surge in youth consumer power. In Western Europe and the United States, the 1950s firmly established young people as a crucial consumer demographic. Shary writes that teenagers' acquisition of cars "gave them new senses of independence and mobility. Now teens no longer had to stay within the confines of their hometown and congregate around a single hangout" (17). The new youth consumer power is troublingly articulated upon the gang's arrival in town: in the tavern, they drink rowdily and to excess, their patronage encouraged by the bar owner, although we know very well what it will lead to. The paternalistic townsfolk's moral panic eventually fixates on Johnny, who is engaged in shedding his tough-guy affectations through his relationship to doe-eyed bartender Kathy (Mary Murphy), who sees in Johnny's mobility the chance to escape her dreary, small-town life.

Structuring the audience's identification more closely around adult authority, one of the most significant films to engage with the unease and increasing visibility of juvenile delinquency was Richard Brooks's adaptation of Evan Hunter's novel *Blackboard Jungle*, which follows the struggle of soft-spoken English teacher Richard Dadier (Glenn Ford) to engage the volatile teenagers of North Manual, an inner-city boys' school. The film opens with an intertitle that makes explicit reference to the public concern over juvenile delinquency, noting its disturbing extension into an otherwise admirably well-meaning school system. However, the film was also denounced from some quarters as part of the problem, partly because of MGM's own marketing, which sensationalized its treatment of delinquency, capitalizing on its shock value (see Golub 25–26). *Blackboard Jungle* opened with Bill Haley and his Comets' "Rock around the Clock," propelling the track to popularity and signaling the cultural ascendance of rock and roll as emblematic of a distinctive and troubling youth culture, imbued with sexuality and rebellion. Comics, too, are part of the problem in the film: Dadier expresses his support for anything that will "get [the students'] minds out of comic books," his role as an English teacher well positioned to counter this apparently toxic non-literature. Ultimately, Dadier is able to get through to his class—including such young talents as Sidney Poitier, Rafael Campos, and Paul Mazursky—after the isolation of bad apple Artie West (Vic Morrow), a villain who epitomizes the insidious influence of gang culture.

Despite its flattering appraisal of a school system that pays tribute to American communities and belief in its young people, *Blackboard Jungle* paints a rather bleaker picture of the state of the American education system in the postwar years. North Manual's teachers are scared, careless, or aggressively cynical (the shop teacher [David Alpert] contemplates assembling a disguised electric chair with which he will immolate his whole class). Adam Golub writes that "Dadier is frustrated by unmotivated students, burned-out colleagues, an unsupportive administration, inadequate school facilities, and an ineffective teacher education program, which he feels did not prepare him to deal with low-achieving students or classroom discipline" (21). In an assembly at the start of the film, the students are barked at via microphone by Mr. Halloran (Emile Meyer), whose manner immediately signals North Manual's pedagogical inferiority in having bred and supported an educator in whom the new teachers struggle to imagine any nurturing or pedagogical spirit: "What does *he* teach?" one questions. In his address, Halloran oscillates between the sarcastic humor of a penal officer and imperatives that clarify his power. Dadier's uncomfortable recollection that Halloran teaches "public speaking or something" contrasts tellingly with the man's frothily indecorous greeting: presumably Halloran has surveyed and quantified his audience and determined that they do not qualify for even a snippet of his elocutionary skill. Childhood, in Brooks's film, is under cynical review. Golub has also persuasively demonstrated that *Blackboard Jungle*, rather than a film merely reflecting the terror of postwar juvenile delinquency, is also symptomatic of what was widely perceived to be a crisis in the education sector: "The idea that schools were in "crisis" first became conventional wisdom in the media in the late 1940s and continued throughout the 1950s" (22). As he points out, a large number of newspapers and magazines had taken to critiquing aspects of the nation's public school system, including its outdated curricula, inadequate infrastructure, and underqualified teachers, along with a worrying surplus of unfilled positions and teachers with low morale (22).

*Blackboard Jungle* also communicates a cultural questioning of children's value that accompanied the baby boom. This notion is perhaps most potently evoked by Richard Dadier's as yet unborn child, carried by his wife, Anne (Anne Francis). Given a recent miscarriage, Anne and Richard are meticulously careful to avoid subjecting Anne to any undue stress. Ostensibly, Anne's forever-endangered body evokes the preciousness and vulnerability of the child—their particular child and the figure of the child more generally. It also helps cements the villainy of problem child Artie, a gang youth who takes to phoning Anne anonymously in order to falsely inform her that her husband is having an affair, behavior that produces in her precisely the kind of mental unbalance that will endanger her child. However, in the context of a film about juvenile delinquency, Anne's pregnancy also encourages us to speculate anxiously on how this precious child might actually turn out. Early in the film, Richard optimistically comments to Anne (and with sexism endorsed at the time) that their child will "have [her] looks and [his] brains and take care of us when we're old." Yet everything to which he bears witness suggests a rude contradiction to their hopes. So troublesome are the film's teenagers, so pervasive is the delinquent subculture they inhabit, that one wonders at the risk involved in even having children. This connection between the delinquent youths and Dadier's unborn child is further evoked by the students' pet name for Dadier: "Daddy-O"—a name spat at him during his final showdown with the villainous Artie.

Brooks's film also gestures with a subtle yet discernable venom to a postwar economy transformed by the employment of women, the kind of workforce change that, as we shall see, became acutely relevant to a number of horror films featuring child villains, from *The Bad Seed* to *The Ring* (2002). "Do I look alright?" opens Lois Hammond (Margaret Hayes), the elegantly dressed teacher beginning the term with Dadier. "Ravishing," replies a colleague who speaks his every remark with a retiring cynicism. "They may even fight over *you*." In her sexual advances on Dadier later in the film, not only does Lois inappropriately infuse the professional sphere with sexuality, but she almost compulsively illustrates her indifference for her job: "Tell me, Richard, don't you ever get fed up with this place? Don't you ever get tired of teaching; don't you feel that you want to throw your briefcase away and take a flyer someplace?—anyplace? With me maybe . . . Don't you? Don't you, Rick?" Dadier's refusal symbolizes not only his dedication to his wife and unborn child but also his thorough passion for teaching. To embrace this woman would be to embrace her defeatist, indifferent attitude to the problems the film depicts. Additionally, Lois's indifference to her work insults the trials of a postwar economy in which male jobs are increasingly occupied by women (the start of the film shows Dadier waiting anxiously among a row of eager applicants).

The students' delinquency is most powerfully illustrated by the attempted rape of Lois in the library after school. Having first flirted mildly with Dadier, to whom she offers a ride home, Lois proceeds down the staircase to wait for him to formally clock out. On the stairs, however, and with a self-conscious glance behind her, she surreptitiously raises her skirt and draws her stockings tighter. Not surreptitiously enough, however, to avoid the voyeuristic gaze of a student (Peter Miller) who lurks at the bottom of the staircase and who—speedily roused by this erotic display—drags her into the deserted library, where she will shortly after be rescued by her desired suitor. In Erving Goffman's terms, Lois's apparently backstage behavior in fixing her stocking has, with worrisome recklessness, been exhibited as front-stage behavior (indeed, a veritable exhibition) for the horny student who lurks in the extreme foreground (see *The Presentation of Self in Everyday Life*). At the moment Lois glances behind her in order to ensure that she is properly outside of Dadier's hopefully admiring gaze, her attacker also pivots self-consciously, ensuring *he* is not under scrutiny. We can see, however, that situated over the railing, the attacker is hardly invisible from Lois's perspective should she choose to actually look. In her preoccupation with her romantic life, this teacher is insufficiently mindful of her audience: a violent boy occupying the central foreground of the shot (just as he and his delinquent buddies should be foremost in any truly professional teacher's awareness in this place). The student is expelled and incarcerated; however, the encounter is framed by a sexist culture that assumes to some extent Lois's complicity in her own attack. The suggestion that Lois somehow asked for what she got is explicitly raised by Dadier's jealous wife but implied more subtly by Lois's preoccupation with her own appearance, carried on against all warnings ("they may even fight over you"), as well as by her continued intermingling of the romantic with the professional in her pursuit of Dadier.

Released the same year that its iconic star, James Dean, would be killed, Nicholas Ray's *Rebel Without a Cause* remains almost certainly the most enduring and influential juvenile delinquent film, exploring with poignancy and uncommon perspective many of the issues that troubled American society about the delinquency scare. *Rebel* begins at the police station's juvenile division, where we are introduced to young trouble-makers Judy (Natalie Wood), Plato (Sal Mineo), and Jim (Dean). On the one hand, Plato's crime of killing puppies represents delinquency's corruption of the innocence and fragility of youth; on the other hand, it prefigures the tragic death of Plato, who is such a tender innocent himself. As Murray Pomerance points out, puppies, rather like Plato, are "soft, big-eyed, emotionally evocative, and in a more or less constant bubble of maternal protection" (59).

Ray's film swiftly traces youth unrest to its social context, including (as in *Blackboard Jungle*) women's new mobility and financial power. The fastidiously social existence of Jim's mother (Ann Doran) is thrust into view when his parents arrive on the scene: white gloved, fur coated, and trailing her own equally gussied-up mother (Virginia Brissac) with her, she rushes toward her son with a concern invested primarily in keeping up appearances. Shary points out that "[Jim's] father is so brow-beaten by Mom that he is effectively emasculated, a domestic crisis born from post-war fears of women's economic liberation" (22). For all his ineptitude, there remains something touching about Jim's father (Jim Backus) in his attempt to connect with the son who is growing up at such a seem-ingly unbridgeable cultural remove; at the police station, he downplays Jim's drinking and fabricates vague narratives of his own youthful jaunts. However, what comes to the fore in the film's first scene (expressed so famously in Dean's eruption, "You're tearing me apart!") is that Jim's parents have no coherent plan for approaching him, but rather vacillate incoherently from one tactic to another. His father pointedly cannot establish for himself an identity apart from his wife's, let alone allow that identity to stand as a model for his son. The juvenile officer fatalistically identifies a broader social problem that lies outside Jim's own negativity, thereby sympathetically normalizing his teenage angst. "How can anyone grow up in a circus like that?" Jim asks him. He responds: "Beats me, Jim, but they do." Conversely, but with equal error, the father (William Hopper) of Jim's future companion, Judy, has a very definitive sense of his daughter's appropriate identity, of how she should present herself and behave. He repels her affections at the dinner table on the basis that she is too old to kiss him, his sense of her proper identity is determined by his knowledge of her emergent sexuality and the social mandate that he repress his attraction to her.

Jim's parents have a history of moving their family around at his mother's behest, nominally in order to safeguard the troubled Jim; however, this behavior also exemplifies the unwillingness of parents to grasp the truly separate and invested social existence of their children. In dislocating their son from his social context, Jim's parents further upset his attempts to position himself in any coherent narrative of self. The family's ceaseless relocation is also used to highlight Jim's mother's obsessive-compulsive focus on impression management—her need to defensively reset and recommence her social persona in response to the slightest potentially embarrassing hiccup. Her indifference to Jim as a social being struggling to fit in is underscored by her hypersensitivity to the ostracizing severity of her own social milieu. The parents of this troubled kid haven't grown up themselves.

Ray's film explores in rich and intricate detail Jim's attempts to integrate himself into the cultural environment of his peers and discover a stable social identity. As he walks into the school building on his first morning there, he unknowingly steps across the institution's emblem etched into the flagstones and is staunchly rebuked by another student for his flagrant disrespect. This moment emblematizes youth culture's abstruse, often indecipherable code of conduct—a code that, in order to foster civil communication (let alone belonging), one must clairvoyantly intuit and faultlessly follow. The difficulty of this endeavor is illustrated more fully during a later scene at the planetarium in the Griffith Park Observatory in which students wisecrack about the show from the safety of the darkness. Despite Jim's having carefully measured and imitated the sophomoric humor of the pranksters around him, the classmates disdain his gag as the work of one not yet initiated. With its narration of the Earth's relative insignificance and inevitable fiery expiration, the planetarium show seems to dwarf the problems that anguish Jim and classmate Plato. However, as Jim's scrunched countenance indicates, the show insults the force of his internal torment—the reality of his cultural milieu and the energy he puts into its observance. As it happens, the urgency of Jim's social existence is illustrated when Buzz (Corey Allen) challenges him to a knife fight outside the planetarium and against a backdrop of the city so overwhelmingly below. In this confrontation (absurdly precipitated by Jim's faux pas but potentially resulting in not mere social but actual death), we see that Jim's social interactions are at the forefront of his emotional, but also physical, existence. As he fights with Buzz, jeered on by a multitude of students, Jim seems truly to be in the stars, the rest of the world having receded to the microscopic.

In the more thoughtful and enduring films of the juvenile delin-quent cycle, one can see not merely historical artifacts of a social scare, but also cinema's ability to treat that uncertainty with circumspection and considerable social insight. While these insights remain (in some cases strongly) inflected by the prejudices of their time, they remain surprisingly sympathetic in their exposition and exploration of the era's challenges to childhood—reflecting with detail on young people's social and psychological complexity and, thus, their personhood. However, it is the passage of these dramatic challenges into the horror genre, their reassembly in a form that repressed rather than interrogated the constructed nature of childhood, that allowed the child villain to become such a trenchant and enduring antagonist.

## Sowing Bad Seeds: Creating the Child as Monster

Emerging into the midst of the juvenile delinquency frenzy was a screen adaptation of William March's 1954 novel *The Bad Seed*, directed by Mervyn LeRoy (and preceded by a Broadway play at the Coronet Theater, Los Angeles, staged by Reginald Denham and featuring the same cast). Released in 1956, *The Bad Seed* provided a disguised yet—because of that disguise—pivotal engagement with the moral panic over juvenile delinquency, situating the child within the lexicon of horror, where her villainy could be unambiguously and lastingly inscribed. Steven Woodward points to the film as "marking the emergence of the child monster in cinema" (305), while Kathy Merlock Jackson stresses that "never before had such an evil image of childhood appeared on the screen" (112). The word "evil" here is crucial in its totality. Rhoda Penmark (Patty McCormack) is a "proper," ladylike child who parades herself in frilly dresses and dainty shoes and has a taste for the material comforts of her class. She also kills a lot of people—transforming the shocking if recognizable (indeed, sympathetic) delinquency of films like *Rebel Without a Cause* or *The Wild One* into irrecoverable villainy.

In *The Bad Seed*, we see in originary form a number of the hallmarks of the child villain film, from immediate successors like 1960's *Village of the Damned* to 2009's *Orphan*. However, in *The Bad Seed*, the broader societal developments surrounding juvenile delinquency, which are consciously explicated in films like *Rebel* and *Jungle* (including gang culture, educational crisis, the spread of mass media, and rock and roll), are strikingly and tellingly absent. The very choice of a young girl as the villain terrifies through its eclipse of familiar delinquent discourse. John Muncie points out that, historically, "[t]he vast majority of criminology theories . . . [had] focussed on *male* offenders, *male* juvenile delinquents and *male* prison populations. . . . Female deviance was largely perceived as relatively insignificant, given women's under-representation in the official crime statistics" (130). Woodward points out that Rhoda's gender undoubtedly works to better conceal her crimes because of the way in which, culturally, "forms of violence are perceived as gendered" (304): not only is Rhoda a child, but she is a girl child, meaning that "the mask of femininity is layered over the mask of childhood" (308). The absence of known signifiers of juvenile delinquency indicates the film's reactionary reembrace of a more recognizable model of childhood focused on innocence and powerlessness—making all the more horrifyingly anomalous the corruption of that model.

For all her gentility, Rhoda, we discover, is the descendent of murderer Bessie Denker, carrier of an innate criminal gene that is undetectable until bloodily evident. This emphasis on a genetic taint is both comforting and confrontational—comforting in the sense that it constructs Rhoda as an aberration that reinforces perceptions of "normal" children and in its confirmation of contemporary child-rearing regimes as faultless; confronting in its suggestion that a bourgeois milieu that disassociates itself from child criminality might still unavoidably be corrupted

Figure 1.1. The dainty child killer, Rhoda Penmark (Patty McCormack), in *The Bad Seed* (Mervyn LeRoy, Warner Bros., 1956), a figure whose horrifying delinquency can only be the result of inherent evil. Digital frame enlargement.

by it (a monster like this can appear anywhere). In the following chapters, I pay special attention to this archetypal child villain's emergence in relation to anxieties surrounding socioeconomic power and a postwar reconsideration of women's social roles. But what deserves immediate note is the film's utter disposal of sympathy for the child and its generalized disregard of social context in its depiction of child delinquency—in effect, its transformation of the juvenile delinquent from a figure of social critique to one of monstrousness.

Partly because of its domestic setting (generally at odds with most 1950s horror) and absence of violence to which the viewer is graphically exposed, *The Bad Seed* is usually treated as a thriller. However, in its removal of monstrosity from the supernatural to the mental, *The Bad Seed* is an early incarnation of what Charles Derry has called the "horror-of-personality" film, exemplified by *What Ever Happened to Baby Jane?* (1962), *Strait Jacket* (1964), and (with incomparable terror and influence on so much of what followed) *Psycho* (1960). Derry points out that while the horror film had traditionally dealt in creations that could be distinguished from the human—physical and metaphysical monstrosities—in the traumatized cultural climate of United States during the 1960s (whose stresses included a rising crime rate, the Kennedy and King assassinations, and the frantically publicized exploits of a number of serial killers), horror villains tended to evoke the violence of the human psyche. In such a context, the ghouls and mad-science concoctions of previous horror cycles seemed to fall into a redundant familiarity. According to Derry, in the 1960s, horror cinema acknowledged that "what *was* horrible . . . was man. It was a horror that was specific, nonabstract, and one that did not need a metaphor. . . . Violence and horror were not explained in terms of science or religion, but in terms of psychology" (24).

Although it predates the tremendous impact of *Psycho*, *The Bad Seed* also roughly coincides with the popularity of the serial killer film, which Peter Hutchings suggests "can be taken as an important vehicle for a fairly broad change occurring in horror from the 1960s onwards, one that involved an increasing stress in the genre on contemporary settings and psychopathological dramas" (53). Like *Psycho*, *The Bad Seed* achieves much of its effect from its location of what is horrifying within what is most cozily familiar, rather than in more remote or Gothic environments (as in *Dracula* [1931] or *The Mummy* [1932]). It attaches horror to a figure at the center of the domestic sphere, the child, moreover (as Woodward points out), the female child. William Paul points out that *The Bad Seed* "effectively brought horror home, domesticating it by locating what is most horrible *within* the family" (270). In this sense, we can see 1960's *Village of the Damned*, which bears the influence of *The Bad Seed*, as a kind of transitional text between old and new forms of horror, a film in the very course of relocating the horrific from the alien to the commonplace. In this film, a group of children are generated by a mysterious extraterrestrial force that impregnates their mothers. That the alien force that plants these bad seeds is never explicitly revealed to us is telling in its indication that the children themselves, in their inexorable power and defiance, are quite frightening enough. The majority of horror films featuring evil children have continued to couch themselves in verisimilitude to the extent of having as their primary loci wholesome country or seaside towns (*The Good Son* [1993], *Village of the Damned*, *Children of the Corn* [1984]) or domestic environments (*It's Alive* [1974], *Rosemary's Baby* (1968), *The Exorcist* [1973]). And despite being a film about apocalyptic prophecy, *The Omen* (1976) declines the use of spectacular effects and subverts any viewer expectation of casual schlock thrills through the dignified presence of a "serious" and domesticated actor, Gregory Peck. For Rick Worland, *Rosemary's Baby* "culminated gothic horror's absorption into the family structure that ran through the decade" (93). This insistence on domestic settings perpetually gestures to and reinforces the ideologically expected (innocent) child, creating an impure and shocking challenge to what we perceive as the natural order of reality.

As I indicated in the introduction to this book, for Noël Carroll, our response to monsters is consistent with a confusion of accepted cultural categories: they are creatures that violate a culture's understanding of natural order, providing us with not merely a physical but also a cognitive threat. Rhoda Penmark's clandestine bloodlust certainly renders her threatening (one of Carroll's criteria for monstrousness); however, more horrifyingly, she is a child who kills. That is, in its categorical violation, the physical threat she presents is utterly eclipsed by the cognitive one. One of the clearest and most enduring categorical impurities enacted by the child villain is his or her generalized transgression of the boundaries between childhood and adulthood. Through their general behavior or speech, child villains uncomfortably lay claim to a disposition confidently circumscribed as adult. In *The Exorcist*, Regan MacNeil (Linda Blair) impresses her mother (Ellen Burstyn) and doctor (Barton Heyman) with an alarming vocabulary of expletives of which, one assumes, she is appropriately and completely unaware; staring downward into the camera, sustaining his gaze so as to properly petrify the cousin who threatens his exposure, the preteen killer of *The Good Son* (1993) flatly instructs: "Don't fuck with me." The boundaries between childhood and adulthood are the subject of such immense sensitivity that we can be shocked and challenged by the child's mere performance of an adult manner. One of the very seriously presented signs that something is wrong with child

Antichrist Damien (Seamus Davey-Fitzpatrick) in John Moore's 2006 remake of *The Omen* is the boy's ability to make himself a perfectly cut sandwich! Rhoda of *The Bad Seed* intolerably confuses the adult with the child in this respect, refusing to wear blue jeans like the other children and preferring prissily adult fashions. As Mrs. Penmark nervously observes, her daughter demonstrates "a mature quality . . . that's disturbing in a child." Carroll points out that the monster's impurity can be structured by fusion, manifested in "a composite that unites attributes held to be categorically distinct and/or at odds in the cultural scheme of things in *unambiguously* one, spatio-temporally discrete entity" (43). While Carroll is speaking primarily of physical fusions, the certainty and cultural investment in the child as a discrete cultural type ensures that its fusion with the adult will provide a similarly monstrous challenge to cultural categories. Rhoda's unnatural status is foregrounded at the film's conclusion when she is struck dead by nothing less than a bolt of lightning—her pollution of the category of child in fact having become so intolerably monstrous that it is corrected from Above.

Although advertisements for the misunderstood teen films certainly exploited fears of contemporary adolescent violence, in the films themselves the viewer's sympathy for the antihero is clearly encouraged and the adult establishment is criticized. As Johnny is tied up and pummeled by villagers in *The Wild One*, he responds with the astonishing line "My old man used to hit harder than that." Christopher Sandford describes Irvin S. Yeaworth's surprise hit *The Blob* (1958), starring soon-to-be icon of 1960s counterculture Steve McQueen as teen savior, as defining "the late fifties morality tale about the small town that refuses to listen to its teenagers" (78). Through the location of fault within a genetic taint, however, *The Bad Seed* laid the foundation of the depiction of future child villain films by reprocessing anxieties over youth culture and the meaning of childhood into more sensational and less sociologically reflective grids of meaning. While its success might have been driven by juvenile delinquent concerns, *The Bad Seed* dislocated its villainy from that context (and any sociological contemplation it might have encouraged) while supercharging its affective force. *The Bad Seed* pushed aside the more sensitive investigations of childhood and purity offered by the most thoughtful of the juvenile delinquent films. Instead, it revived and relied on the image of the innocent child by brutally contradicting it. In this way, *The Bad Seed* potently transferred to future depictions of children what Joann Conrad, writing on children in the media, has called the "Janus-faced, good/evil" character (185). According to Conrad, through "the dual image of the innocent angel/monstrous child, adults attempt to segregate 'good children' from those 'bad children' who dispel the fantasy of the perfect child" (185). The film's status as horror is wrapped up with sensitivity to the cultural category of childhood, the extremity of reaction provoked by its pollution. Horror cinema has continued to be the most effective domain for challenges to the idea of the innocent child, challenges that nevertheless reinforce this volatile category.

Providing a more reflective depiction of children anchored in innocent/evil binaries was Jack Clayton's thriller *The Innocents* (1960), which, despite finding its source material in Henry James's 1898 novella *The Turn of the Screw*, neatly complemented the cinematic reassessment of childhood that occurred during the postwar era. Miss Giddens (Deborah Kerr) is employed in her first role as the governess of Miles (Martin Stephens) and Flora (Pamela Franklin), the two young wards of a wealthy, unnamed uncle who finds his lifestyle incompatible with their care. The two children begin to steadily contradict the innocent characterization their new governess had adoringly imagined. Eventually, she becomes convinced that they are possessed by the spirits of the valet and his mistress, the previous governess—a couple given to scandalous sexual encounters within the house itself and presumably within view or hearing of the children. As Merlock Jackson writes, the film "addresses some growing questions of its time. Are we a society that is losing its innocence? Do we expect our children to be better, more innocent than they possibly can be?" (133). The film shows several hallmarks of the child villain, such as distinctive precociousness and an especially uncanny adult speech that unnervingly challenges the adult-child hierarchy—children who speak to their adult interlocutors as intellectual equals or even inferiors. While one hesitates to characterize the children of this film as villains, *The Innocents* partakes of a similarly binary reading of the child. Clayton's film adapts and amplifies the insinuation in James's novella that the specters the governess sees are an expression of her own repressed sexual desire for the children's absent uncle, along with her obsessive desire to protect the children from sexual contamination. Right up to its conclusion, Clayton's film refuses to clarify whether the children's "possession" is not simply a construction of the governess's fear that they have somehow been polluted by the sexuality of the former residents. So unwavering is her angelic vision of the children that compromises to it can be understood by her only as the effects of foreign spiritual forces.

While not as influential as *The Bad Seed*, *The Innocents* demonstrates the positioning of the child within the binary readings the earlier film sets up. The difference is that whereas *The Innocents* encourages the viewer to reflect on the constructed, projected, and potentially overdetermined nature of childhood through the governess's potential insanity, *The Bad Seed* constructs its villain as a perverse aberration of an ideal and stable innocence that is taken for granted. It is, however, the perverted innocent, and the terrible tension he or she inspires, that took hold in horror films to come.

## Conclusion

Shary writes that "by the early 1960s, the public's and the studios' interest in juvenile delinquents had waned, at least for the type of JDs that disrupted school and threatened their parents" (26). Yet concern over juvenile delinquency continued into the 1960s and 1970s, augmented by public worry over the emergence of a hippie counterculture. Writing in 1975, Ruth Cavan and Theodore Ferdinand observed that "[i]n spite of the fact that the proportion of juveniles in the population has been declining since 1970, the percentage who engage in delinquency has continued to increase . . ." (6). Kincheloe notes that "by the end of the 1970s headlines such as 'Killer Kids' and newspaper copy such as 'Who are our children? One day they are innocent. The next, they may try to blow your head off' had made an impact. No more assumptions about innocence, no more surprises" (165). William Paul loosely attributes later films to the troubling visibility of youth culture in the 1960s and 1970s. For him, a film like *The Omen* "confirms a sense of the child as being actually alien to its family," and he notes that "this truth seems to have particular resonance for this period" (326). By this era, anxiety over youth had been funneled into a cinematic form, where it could continue to alarm the social scene with challenges to definitions of childhood while evading reflection on the constructed nature of childhood itself.

In contrast with the teenagers of the juvenile delinquent film, many of whom were played by often irrepressibly adult actors, the child villain in *The Bad Seed* is far less ambiguously a child, and this fact assisted in amplifying the film's disruption of childhood into the horrific. The transformation of children rather than teenagers into monsters was also crucial to the child villain film's perpetuation in light of horror films' substantial teenage audience. In consumer culture, that teen audience was a powerful bloc. *Blackboard Jungle* clearly pinpoints a few thoroughly bad apples within a cluster of contemporary youth; however, as Leerom Medovoi has explained, the film is also subject to oppositional readings that celebrate the volatile youth culture and rebellion that it ostensibly vilifies. For Medovoi, the opening scene's irresistible use of "Rock around the Clock" enlists young audiences against adult authority, presenting "a moment when the implied viewer is most clearly a youth who rocks to the music of delinquency" (158). But if young people became a key cinema demographic in the 1950s, with teens rushing to see juvenile delinquent films and accommodating their representations through a variety of interpretive postures, the effect of the child villain in horror hinged on his or her construction as thoroughly and intolerably Other. Abstracted out of the social context of juvenile delinquency, the child, in whom the hopes of the status quo are invested, was able to play host to a large variety of anxieties—anxieties we now examine in more detail, beginning with *The Bad Seed* and *Village of the Damned*.

# 2

## Spoiled Rotten

### Horror's Bourgeois Brats

B AD CHILDREN ARE RARELY BROUGHT up badly—or not in the movies, anyway. As Sabine Büssing points out, in the horror genre, where child villains thrive, children overwhelmingly appear as either victims or victimizers (xvi); they do not appear as both, and the most intolerable children—far from being casualties of domestic torment— come from well-to-do homes. Among these well-bred brats we count the various children of the various *Village of the Damned* films, with their tidy haircuts and haughty accents; iconic child menace Damien of *The Omen* is the son of an ambassador; the straitlaced and soft-spoken child in *Whisper* (2007) is held hostage for his family's money before he begins seriously spooking his captors. The child demon in low-budget thriller *Demonic Toys* (1992) goes as far as sipping from a glass of red wine. In *Joshua* (2007), the formally dressed, piano-playing son of a New York stockbroker threatens to literalize his social privilege when, with shocking matter-of-factness, he responds to a vagrant's appeal for money with a proposition: "I'll give you five dollars if I can throw a rock at you."

While he does not wear elite dress, the entitlement of Henry (Macaulay Culkin) of *The Good Son* (1993) is a crucial component of his villainy, as he delights in tormenting a dockworker's pit bull and vandal- izing the man's rundown shed, while his evil remains so long undetected because of his affluent family background. Socioeconomic superiority

Figure 2.1. Proper dress, improper thoughts: the privileged child psychopath (Jacob Kogan) of *Joshua* (George Ratliff, Twentieth Century Fox, 2007). Digital frame enlargement.

is chillingly pronounced in the zombie film *Resident Evil* (2002), which repackages the dubious supercomputer of films such as *2001: A Space Odyssey* (1968) by anthropomorphizing it as a primly dressed, English-accented young girl named "The Red Queen" (Michaela Dicker). This dainty little imp presides over a capitalist endeavor that indifferently sacrifices its workers; the use of a child as a symbol of exploitation is strengthened in this case by the inhuman rationality of artificial intelligence. This particular icon is expensive, thus tonally elevated in class, as well as disdainfully obnoxious. As perhaps the most enduring and recognizable profile for the child villain, the posh brat has traveled far into other genres, demonstrating the force of children as impertinent representatives of socioeconomic power. Draco Malfoy (Tom Felton), the bullying, platinum-haired schoolyard nemesis of Harry Potter (Daniel Radcliffe) in the celebrated series of books and films, draws on the spotless and intolerably stately characterizations developed in horror, pompously announcing his privilege in film after film, particularly in contrast to Harry's hard-up chum Ron Weasley (Rupert Grint).

In a number of iconic and exemplary horror films, we see a consistent and enduring preoccupation with social status in the depiction of child villainy—children who seem to suppose they have some terrible and divinely derived entitlement to kill. In this chapter, I want to consider in more detail why this bourgeois brat has become a standard expression of childhood evil in film through a study of two films crucial to standardizing the theme: that landmark of child villainy, *The Bad Seed* (1956); and Wolf Rilla's 1960 adaptation of *Village of the Damned* from the novel by John Wyndham. Our frequently adopted view of children as "natural," innocent, and pure conceals ideologically motivated definitions, values, and programs of action—the programs we consider most desirable and worthy of continuation with respect to children (and the ones that, when faultlessly reflected back to us, are then mistaken as part of the child's "natural" state). The "ideal" characteristics and values we ask children to introject and reflect back to us inevitably construct as undesirable those who do not observe those values or have those characteristics. In teaching children how to "properly" present themselves according to the standards of bourgeois society, we reaffirm the unacceptability or inferiority of those who, as adults, are not to us so "proper." Thus, embedded in what we project onto and encourage in children are ideals that imply and perpetuate social hierarchy and oppression. The following explores the way in which villainous children who draw explicitly on the language of class horrifyingly expose political inequalities embedded within constructions of what we would otherwise take to be "perfect" children.

## Killing with Class: *The Bad Seed*

No child was ever spoiled quite so rotten as Rhoda Penmark (Patty McCormack). Pretty and prissy, tailored and tidy, mannered to reflect her affluence, and apparently the perfect old-fashioned little lady, Rhoda is the delight of her military father (William Hopper) and the landlady Mrs. Breedlove (Evelyn Varden), a flamboyant divorcee and amateur psychoanalyst, both of whom lavish gifts upon her. Yet when Rhoda can't have something she wants, she thinks little of using murder to acquire it. After little Claude Daigle, the precocious child of a working-class family, is found drowned, Rhoda falls under suspicion of snatching his penmanship prize—later sought as a memento by the boy's distraught mother. Rhoda's own mother, Christine (Nancy Kelly), discovers the medal concealed beneath the lining of her daughter's "treasure chest." Perturbed by Rhoda's emphatic remorselessness ("Claude didn't need the medal: Claude was *dead*!"), Christine sets about quizzing a journalist friend on the ins and outs of child criminality. She seeks especially to confirm killer kids as the products of bad parenting (cases of nurture over nature), thereby ruling out her doted-on daughter. Yet, to her horror, the friend informs her that there also exists a type of criminal who was "born evil," irrespective of upbringing and social influence, and impervious to rehabilitation: the kind of "bad seed" whom Rhoda so stunningly appears to exemplify. Having now realized that she is herself, in fact, the daughter of notorious vamp Bessie Denker, a nurse who murdered her patients, Christine deduces that she must be carrying some latent criminal gene now active inside her deadly daughter. Under her mother's questioning, Rhoda eventually fesses up to Claude's murder: she told this (according to her) quite undeserving winner to hand over his prize, and when he refused, she hammered him in the head with the metal heel of her shoe and shoved him into the lake. As Christine anxiously shilly-shallies, the cunning Rhoda also murders the janitor, Leroy (Henry Jones), whose petty mockery of her has given way to genuine suspicion. The girl's killing streak is abated only by streak of lightning that zaps her dead at the film's conclusion.

The Bad Seed is of pointed and enduring interest given its contribution of the term "bad seed" to popular culture—as a means by which we might imagine childhood evil as something innate and irreparable. The frequency with which the term is called upon in casual conversation or journalism related to child criminality seems to suggest that the film and the novel from which it was adapted hit upon and articulated an already existing popular suspicion of a culturally unspecific, transcendentally rotten, inherent, or "inherited" variety of badness (see Petley, Jackson). Indeed, Stephani Etheridge Woodson points out that contemporary reviews referred to the "numbing plausibility" and "disturbing realism" of the Rhoda Penmark character (34). This praise of "realism," however, conceals a willingness to excuse the accusing adult of responsibility for the malfunction of his or her otherwise most valued ideological project: the child. As I have earlier suggested, The Bad Seed's stunning vision of "inherent" evil imbued numerous later depictions of child villainy. Certainly the film's dramatic deus ex machina confirms Rhoda's evil as demonically inborn; nevertheless, closer analysis gives us a villainy profoundly contextualized by socioeconomic division. "Haven't you ever heard of 'spoiling someone?'" Christine chides Breedlove in the film's opening scene after the landlady gives Rhoda jewelry and a pair of ominously dark sunglasses studded with rhinestones. As Rhoda's ominous gaze (newly blackened in a fusion of ruthlessness and materialism) indicates, she is indeed *spoiled* rotten, the product of social action and hardly just an indiscriminate genetic anomaly. It is through her material rather than inherent corruption that much of the film's horror is conjured.

The Bad Seed abounds with signifiers of class hierarchy. Early in the film, for example, Leroy the janitor is reprimanded for walking directly through the family home. More obviously, we bear witness (with responses varying from bemusement to horror) to Rhoda's materialism: her absurd tantrum over failing to acquire something she didn't earn (the penmanship medal) and her suggestion that she had offered Claude fifty cents to wear the medal for the day. We also recognize the nature of her victims: the poor Claude Daigle, and boorish dogsbody Leroy. The insistence of Mrs. Penmark's friend that a special kind of killer may start early, just as "Mozart showed his melodic genius at eight," prefigures a scene in which Rhoda practices piano loudly in order to cover up the dying screams of Leroy, but it also uncomfortably associates murderousness with the refined tastes of the bourgeoisie. As the drunk Hortense Daigle (Eileen Heckart) bursts into the Penmark home, the film's focus on class bursts from the subtext and into clear view. Hortense arrives ostensibly to question Rhoda as the last person to see her son alive, yet she cannot help but snap at Christine: "You're a superior person. . . . I bet you made a début and everything!" For Hortense, the death of her son is not only a deep trauma, permitting her to dispense with social decorum by arriving drunk, but (even before she knows the details) somehow yet *another* instance of her social hardship and oppression, an event that further licenses her confrontation of the privileged Christine.

The viewer of *The Bad Seed* is ushered into the film through narrative strategies that construct our response to Rhoda as a disturbing aberration of a class-specific ideal: that is, her crimes are made more shocking because of our acceptance and implicit endorsement of the civilized and "proper" home from which she comes. The film restricts us to the bourgeois environs of the Penmark house: the opening shots take us from the stormy jetty (where Rhoda will eventually be struck dead) to the stability of their affluent home, through which the tones of Rhoda's piano practice charmingly drift. The narrative point of view also prioritizes wealthy homemaker Christine as protagonist in the wake of her husband's absence, with the shock of Rhoda's transgressions expressed through her.

An early scene provides an especially powerful means of harmonizing the viewer's and Christine's perspectives and implicitly acclimatizing us to her classed milieu. The "accident" at the school picnic that leads to Claude Daigle's death is initially reported via a radio broadcast that fails to name the child involved. Because the viewer has by this time already been introduced to Rhoda (who has not yet flaunted her monstrosity), the suspicion, voiced by Christine, is that the victim is the young girl herself. As viewers share Christine's distress, so too they feel her uneasy relief when it becomes clear that it was not Rhoda after all but young Claude, the "only child of Mr. and Mrs. Henry Daigle." Thank goodness for that. The suffering of those outside the Penmark domain is thus swept aside for the moment with a relief later to be challenged by the unexpected intrusion of the working-class Mr. and Mrs. Daigle into both the narrative and the Penmark family home. Similarly, prior to his murder by Rhoda, the janitor Leroy creepily wanders into our view, saddled with disaffection and potential menace: he is framed, first, by the Penmark conception of him. Thus, *The Bad Seed* both brings class hierarchy to the fore and at least initially encourages us to accept a position on the upper rungs of the ladder, confining us to the bourgeois perspective that Rhoda will so thoroughly alarm.

Observing the film's preoccupation with a kind of idealized, bourgeois domestic sphere, Chuck Jackson focuses on social division primarily in terms of Rhoda's privileged whiteness—a significant part of her social dominance. For Jackson, the horror presented by Rhoda is directly linked to the unreadability of her whiteness, an attribute usually associated with purity and goodness. He focuses on the degree to which an idealized white cuteness is presented through Rhoda as a disturbingly "performable aesthetic." For Jackson, the idea that an idealized, domestic, white purity can be "performed" threatens to unravel the validity of the "cultural ideal and American dream" of "the safe, white, bourgeois home of the 1950s" (71). Thus, what is most significant for Jackson is the murderous Rhoda's ultimate status as a performer: a pretender to the values she seems to physically represent (cuteness, whiteness, domesticity, bourgeois sensibility). Rhoda is a performer all right (performing emotional responses, performing innocence), yet there is nothing to suggest that she "performs"—and thus has no genuine relationship to—her bourgeois status (or its valued whiteness). She performs the qualities typically associated with bourgeois whiteness, but not bourgeois whiteness itself. In fact, the sincerity of her bourgeois tastes is immoderately pronounced. Early in the film we see that Rhoda, with no motive for saying so, does not consider blue jeans quite "ladylike" enough; that she enjoys playing piano; that she delights in and fetishizes material possessions. Jackson's perspective also overlooks the specific nature of Rhoda's victims: the stooped and churlish janitor and the underprivileged Claude Daigle. In short, what we are seeing in Rhoda is not merely a performance of bourgeois ideals that threatens to render those ideals empty in themselves (a simulacrum that, as Baudrillard would have it, threatens our trust in an original truth), but a staggering display of Rhoda's social power—the bourgeoisie's improper performance and vulgar exposure of its own superiority. Rhoda is the bourgeois child in extremis—terribly revealing a cultural superiority and entitlement that should, ideally, remain unannounced, physically unenforced, and thus apparently consensual.

The idea that Rhoda audaciously announces a superiority that ought to remain hidden is prefigured early in the film, when she flips her lid over Claude's winning the penmanship medal: "Everyone said I wrote the best hand, and I should have had it! I just don't see how Claude Daigle got the medal." Christine's consolation is telling: "Rhoda, these things happen to us all the time . . . And when they do we simply accept them." Crucially, her mother does not actually deny that Rhoda was the more worthy candidate (indeed, the family's surname, Penmark, suggests her "natural" entitlement to the prize). Christine thus effectively validates Rhoda's complaint, merely attempting to moderate the baldness of its expression. What is at issue here is not Rhoda's sense of entitlement but her unseemly presentation of it—that she does not behave in a way that graciously conceals her "natural" dominance. She may in fact consider herself superior, more worthy, but she must not—under any circumstances—actually *say so*. Similarly, most confrontational in Hortense Daigle's intrusion into the Penmark home is her blunt assertion that Christine is "a superior person" to her. Christine is perfectly aware of the differences between Hortense Daigle and herself, yet Hortense treats her to a brutal and accusatory illustration of that difference. In her tirade, social power hideously emerges from its consignment to the silent, the mannered, and the invisible—a return of the repressed that Rhoda's crimes repeat and appallingly amplify.

The child is of course a locus of social conditioning, a site of ideological investment for the future, and this means that he or she is also situated to provide an idealized reflection of the status quo. Through her contrived presentation, her proud display of the signs of bourgeois privilege, we can see in Rhoda an entrustment—even a proud emblem—of class-specific social values. However, the dominant association of childhood with innocence and naturalness means that those values are conventionally as disguised as they are promoted. In Rhoda's shocking crimes, however, which do not so much conflict with as horrifyingly complement her class status, social hierarchy is made hideously literal. Rhoda's fellow humans, especially those socially "lower," exist for her as mere resources for exploitation. Her behavior explosively dramatizes social inequality, horribly confronting us with what must remain veiled and thus uninterrogated for inequality to be successfully perpetuated. The question posed by Rhoda's behavior—how could a good child go so wrong?—is of course resolved by the thesis that identifies her as the product of a genetic rather than social taint. Her bourgeois tastes and character are thus constructed as irrelevant to her murderousness, her social milieu saved from the stigma of criminality. Yet in this child we see the bourgeoisie's fear of its own ordinarily hidden predacity and violence.

The ideological dimension to Rhoda's "childish innocence"—as a quality expressing and idealizing systems of power—is illustrated by her interaction with the boorish Leroy. Exempt from the bourgeois values that Rhoda so gaudily represents, Leroy insolently refuses to regard her as cute or innocent: "You don't puzzle me none, little Miss Sweet-Lookin'," he slurs, getting closer than he realizes to the truth of Claude's death. "You're smart. . . . But I'm smarter." For Leroy, Rhoda's "smart-ness" is contained in her ability to perfectly express (even exaggerate) bourgeois civility as a way of confirming her girlish innocence. However, if Rhoda's prissy mannerisms mean she can manipulate her parents and teachers, Leroy is immune because he is subversively dislocated from those conventions: Rhoda is not so innocent because, in his view, neither are all those prim postures, in Rhoda or anyone else.

At its conclusion, *The Bad Seed* emphatically reconfirms childhood as an apolitical site of innocence and vulnerability through the deus ex machina that destroys Rhoda. The bolt of lightning constructs her as an aberration of an empirical childhood: a freak of nature rather than anything for which society, or individual adults, could conceivably bear

Figure 2.2. "You don't puzzle me none, little Miss Sweet-Lookin": the working-class Leroy (Henry Jones) is not bewitched by the ladylike stylings of killer kid Rhoda Penmark (Patty McCormack) in Mervyn LeRoy's *The Bad Seed* (Warner Bros., 1956). Digital frame enlargement.

responsibility. This "anomalous" infection of the bourgeoisie is cleanly deleted. Despite the film's final, quaint request that viewers not give away the "daring" conclusion to those yet to watch it, *The Bad Seed*'s ideas about childhood are, ultimately, urgently conservative. Rhoda is defensively reconstructed as not just culturally unacceptable but utterly anomalous: comfortably immune from the socioeconomic power the film has used to enflame anxiety all along.[1] Nevertheless, this discursive shift fails to wholly exorcise the feeling that Rhoda is not inherently bad but *spoiled* rotten: the ideological distillation of a culture willing to assign superiority where it has not been earned.

## Heirs Aberrant: *Village of the Damned*

Wolf Rilla's *Village of the Damned* bears some similarity to *The Bad Seed* in its evocation of class difference, pursuing the same narrative preference for the wealthier classes and visually establishing its child villains in conjunction with that social stratum. The small, semirural Midwich becomes the sleepiest of sleepy little villages when every life form within its boundaries suddenly and synchronously loses consciousness. Upon awakening hours later, the female residents discover themselves pregnant, eventually birthing a legion of fair-haired and preternaturally bright brats whose paternity we can only attribute to the same, invisible intergalactic force that caused the village's sudden slumber. Once sufficiently grown, the children march around town in a pompous blond brigade, capable not only of reading minds but also of telepathically controlling their opposers—pinioning them with an unnervingly luminous stare and directing them to self-harm (an especially striking motif whose full implications I discuss in the following chapter).

The film opens with a relaxed pan along a lightly wooded stretch of English countryside, accompanied by the romantic strains of harp and oboe. A small herd of sheep trot across the grounds of the opulent Kyle Manor, driven by a groundskeeper from the path of a tractor. This dreamily innocuous depiction of working-class labor prefigures a gentle fade to the interior of the manor. The master of the house, Professor Gordon Zellaby (George Sanders), strolls past an open fire on his way to the telephone. He makes a call to inquire after a book, an action important for the story only in that it evokes a person at the other end of the line and thus sets up the outside world's knowledge of something amiss in Midwich, because the professor suddenly faints mid-conversation. In the following scenes, the film affects a documentary style: the soundtrack is reduced to the strictly diegetic as a series of detached, matter-of-fact pans detail the chaotic disruptions to Midwich life produced by the village-wide siesta, or "Dayout" (as Wyndham's novel terms it) at a number of miscellaneous locations.

This opening, intended to portray normal life in Midwich prior to the interference, works by prioritizing a distinctly bourgeois sense of regularity. While it imparts to the viewer that the working classes have also been affected, these glimpses are offered more in the spirit of further scrutiny, topical detail about the immediate, higher-level disruption exemplified by Zellaby's sudden collapse. Our focus on the privileged is retained and reinforced once the villagers awaken. As the suave and tweedy professor ventures into town, we are neatly aligned with him against a gaggle of inquisitive and agitated working folk. He is first detained by a shopkeeper, for whose ignorant hypothesizing he clearly has no time but feels obliged to gently curtail, particularly as she complains that those in power are somehow "trying to pull the wool over our eyes." Zellaby placates her through condescension: "Tell you what," he says, swifting the simple gossipmonger aside, "I'll press for an official explanation while you help to stop the rumors getting about, all right?" A moment later, a housewife starts on the same disaffected line: "The least they can do is offer us some kind of compensation!" Her grumbling is subdued by her husband's mollifying but inane interruption: "What the wife means is, well!—you don't hardly expect to drop asleep before dinner, do ya!" Outside the earshot of these curious but solidly unremarkable folks, Zellaby easily cozies up to the official investigation, becoming one of its crucial advisers by virtue of his education and social standing, the narrative henceforth framed from his relatively lofty perspective. Whatever is going on in Midwich, we can trust that if anyone will get a handle on it, it'll be the upper middle class.

The mysterious pregnancies first appear to harmonize the social strata of Midwich, given that they affect women of all backgrounds and classes: the affluent Zellabys' announcement that they are expecting is juxtaposed with that of a distraught virgin with neither financial nor marital support. However, the children, once born, amass as an arrogantly "superior" class of their own, bearing all the (white supremacist) signifiers of cultural and racial superiority: platinum blond hair, aristocratic accents, formal clothing, and a demeanor that condescendingly substitutes extraordinary formality and poise for outward aggression. At their birth, a doctor pronounces them physically "perfect in every respect."

The children articulate their goals in broadly Darwinist terms: they will subjugate their parents through natural superiority. However, the Darwinist thesis (allowed more explicit expression in John Carpenter's 1995 remake) wears all the signifiers of socioeconomic power play. Professor Zellaby here righteously emblematizes the ruling class, and in the

Figure 2.3. "Perfect in every respect": the genteel child invaders of Wolf Rilla's *Village of the Damned* (Warner Bros., 1960). Digital frame enlargement.

1995 film, his equivalent, Dr. Alan Chaffee (Christopher Reeve), is the one to get the news that (clever and respected fellow though he may be) he will be "dominated." In both films, the town's social dignitaries must reckon with a force that threatens to humiliate their authority and transform them (as, Marx showed, the bourgeoisie has long transformed workers) into a mere resource for exploitation.

Whereas *The Bad Seed* resolved Rhoda's threat to the bourgeoisie by isolating and removing her as an "intruder," *Village of the Damned* restates the importance and priority of its ruling classes through a combination of intellectual triumph and Christlike sacrifice. Zellaby brings to his meeting with the children a product of his own genius—a homemade time bomb—intending to blow the invaders up even at the cost of losing his own life. With titanic mental strain, Zellaby blocks the children's telepathy for long enough to ensure the bomb explodes. This bloody conclusion is somewhat incongruous given Zellaby's earlier discouragement of a working-class villager who was bent on gunning the children down in the street. The lofty professor's death—so that others may live—is nobly sacrificial, whereas the working-class deaths that lead up to it seriatim are mere by-the-way frighteners. The film's preoccupation with intelligence means that the intellectual children must be ranged against someone comparable: if these children are going to be murdered, it is because they are going to be *outsmarted*, the "crudeness" of murder allayed by a demonstration of superior reason. In the films of both Rilla and Carpenter, the final scene takes the form of an intellectual "showdown" where the protagonists and villains stare intensely at each other in a telepathic tug-of-war: a literal battle of the minds. In the struggle for social dominance, the murder of the children is a triumphant reassertion of the rights and glory of the middle class. Zellaby's Christlike immolation also underscores the essential "humanity" of the bourgeoisie, its capacity and willingness to suffer (and that it *does* suffer), while spectacularizing bourgeois suffering as remarkable and transcendental. Further and further from our thoughts is cast the quotidian suffering that the machinations of capitalism inflict on the powerless and render routine and invisible. In the conclusion to both films occurs not only the restoration of the ruling intellectual classes, but an assurance of their irretractable importance to the social order.

Ostensibly, *Village of the Damned* intends to provoke the suggestion of a "generation war" or anxieties over rebellious youth (as befits a film produced in the wake of a cultural panic over juvenile delinquency). In reality, though, the Midwich children are neither "wild" nor out of control. The problem is that their rationality belittles the adults' sense of control and apparently superior intellect. Like *The Bad Seed*, *Village of the Damned* provides a compelling example of the child's function of providing feelings of adults' social belonging and dominance, specifically through the crisis instigated when that function is refused. Zellaby's dreams for his son, whom he hopes will be "the next Einstein" or "perhaps even greater" (perpetuating and amplifying the father's intellectual dominance and social status), are appallingly inverted: the shining junior will not perpetuate and affirm his father's intellect but threaten to humiliate it. A hierarchically superior "class" is implied by the children's behavior, mannerisms, intellect, and appearance—one to which the current ruling classes are abruptly, inexplicably denied access. The Dayout children are not equalizers repairing inequality between the existing social strata; rather, they thrust those in power horrifyingly downward.

## Conclusion

Class antagonism has been a generally overlooked preoccupation of the horror film, although some scholars have brought it into the light. For example, Barry Keith Grant's 1996 essay "Rich and Strange" discusses a group of films from the mid-1980s onward to which he applies the label "yuppie horror." Some of these, such as *The Hand That Rocks The Cradle* (1992), would at first seem to fit more within the spectrum of thriller or drama than "horror," and some, such as *Desperately Seeking Susan* (1985) and *Something Wild* (1986), within neither. Yet Grant perspicaciously argues that "the fears and anxieties of the yuppie subculture . . . encourage the transformation of 'evil' in these movies from the classic horror film's otherworldly supernatural to the material and economic pressures of this world that is too much with us" (155). These films depict the torment of sympathetic middle-to-upper-class protagonists through the tenuousness of economic privilege, entertaining, for example, "the premise of the descent by middle-class characters into the hell of the inner city" or the "seeming oxymoron of the terrible luxury home" as an update on the conventional horror trope of the haunted house (156). More recently, the "yuppie horror" cycle was brought back in revised form with films such as *American Psycho* (2000) and *Hostel* (2005), which cast the security and personal autonomy of the rich as the attacking Other rather than the subject of attack and evoke anxiety over how excessive social power might be exerted physically. Both victim/aggressor arrangements at least implicitly question the hegemony of capitalism and its excesses. What I have called the bourgeois brat provides a powerful manifestation of these themes, intertwined with, and unsettlingly obscured by, the discourses that inform putatively empirical conceptualizations of the child. While wearing all the ordinarily endorsed signs of social privilege, the children of *The Bad Seed* and *Village of the Damned* enact that privilege with terrifying force. What's more, in doing so, they bring to light how much what we value about and encourage in the child is rooted in inequality.

# 3

## A Scary Sight

### The Looking Child

"**B**EWARE THE EYES THAT PARALYZE!!!"; "What demon force lurks behind those eyes?"; "Beware the stare that will paralyze the will of the world" . . . So ran a series of taglines for Wolf Rilla's *Village of the Damned* (1960), motifs from which have been borrowed and processed into clichés of popular film and television over several decades. Novelists and filmmakers alike have used the image of a staring child to convey a mysterious and disarming refusal of adult power, something beyond the implausibility (or banality) of physical opposition. In *The Turn of the Screw*, the governess receives her spookily hostile ward Flora's first flash of outright resistance primarily through her look, noting that "the singular reticence of our communion was even more marked in the frank look she launched me" (102). Posters for *The Good Son* (1993) suggested the maliciousness of its child villain (Macaulay Culkin) through his poisonously green squint. "I heard that the eyes are the windows to the soul," remarks an abducted eight-year-old boy (Blake Woodruff) in *Whisper* (2007) before his own eyes are flooded with black, revealing that he is in fact a demon in disguise. In the supernatural thriller *The Unborn* (2009), a young woman (Odette Yustman) is spooked by a wan-faced phantom child (Ethan Cutkosky) with luminous blue eyes. This chapter considers the antagonism of the looking child with particular reference to three films in which this theme is anxiously centralized: *Village of the Damned*, its 1995 remake by John Carpenter, and *Halloween* (1978), also directed by Carpenter. In all three, we receive powerfully focused representations of the child's gaze as a disruptive force, representations that can be analyzed to reveal a great deal about the way children are conceptualized by adults and how this conceptualization is dependent on the child presenting him- or herself in a particular way for our adult gaze. I discuss the child's evil or empowered gaze as a subversion of the stable and received understandings of childhood that are maintained by the way children are ordinarily looked *at*; wrapped up in the spectacle of the malevolently gazing child is an upheaval of the comforting passivity the adult expects.

The murder with which *Halloween* sensationally commences is depicted entirely through the eyes of the young boy who perpetrates it. This is a point of view keenly emphasized in the moments leading up to the act by the restrictive eyeholes of a Halloween mask and one that is fundamental in positing his eyes as agents of evil themselves. Later in the film, a psychiatrist's recollection of the boy centralizes his eyes as the crucial signifier of his villainy: this child had "the blackest eyes—the devil's eyes." When this killer kid reappears ten years later, all grown up, he sports a white mask, featureless except for its cavernously black eye sockets, which menacingly obscure from us the demonic eyes within. Thus, the villain's psychopathy is announced partly by his inscrutable line of sight—the fact that he could, at any moment, be looking anywhere (or everywhere).[1] The opening scene, though—which is my focus here—conveys a remarkable upheaval of the expectations of childhood rooted in the relationship between seeing and power. Similarly, in *Village of the Damned*, in which children actually destroy adults through the power of their gaze, the conspicuously gazing child presents a challenge to culturally recognized models of childhood. Both films use the look to troublingly present children as "subjects" rather than "objects," spooking us with their intolerable independence.

## An Uncertain Zoom:
## Power and Perspective in *Halloween*

*Halloween* stirs to life with the sound of children reciting a rhyme (composed for the film) that pays tribute to Halloween iconography (black cats, ghosts and goblins) and concludes with the chorus "Trick or treat!" An insert informs us of the setting in more detail: (the fictional) Haddonfield, Illinois; Halloween night, 1963. What follows is a scene that deserves more than a little attention. Despite the multitude of voices to which we have just been listening, we see no children onscreen. Instead, a Steadicam shot moves across a quiet suburban street and toward a two-story house, its gentle bounce indicating that we are experiencing someone's point of view. Through the glass panel of the closed front door, this mystery viewer spies a couple of teenagers smoochily groping each other. "My parents won't be home until ten," the girl assures as the couple disappears from view. In order to keep this amorous duo in his sights, the peeper maneuvers to the side of the house, obtaining a view of the two clambering and caressing on the couch in the living room. Still from outside the house, we hear the boy (having received confirmation of prolonged parental absence) press forward: "Let's go upstairs." The girl assents, and the randy couple bounds up the staircase toward a bedroom, the boy's hands already venturing beneath his lover's skirt as he chases her. The stalker—for so he plainly seems—doubles back to his original vantage point and gazes upward to see the upstairs light switch off. This sign of the couple's sexual engagement is accompanied by an eerie synth tingle that ensures we recognize that while they invest their giddy attention in each other, they are easy prey for this lurking menace: earlier, the young man had paused mid-grope to question the girl, "We are alone, aren't we?" "Michael is around somewhere," she nonchalantly noted before they got back to business (whoever this Michael is, he hardly warrants a serious thought).

Perhaps an opportunistic burglar, perhaps a jilted lover incensed by his beloved's now consummate betrayal, the peeper swiftly moves around to the back of the house and slips in through the open back door. Moving through the kitchen, he switches on a light, then lingers briefly in the kitchen. A brightly colored arm reaches forth, opening a drawer and grasping a cook's knife; the weapon is quickly withdrawn beyond the frame, poised for forceful (and fatal) thrusts. He continues to move through the house, pausing briefly before the dining table, as if recognizing it as the key symbol of the family home whose sanctity his intrusion violates; he then stops at the couch on which the teenagers were recently groping. At the foot of the stairs nearby we hear a voice, although not that of our still-mysterious peeper: "Look Judy, it's really late—I gotta go." After creeping toward the stairs up which the young lovers playfully dashed, the intruder suddenly withdraws slightly in order to avoid detection by the young man—now descending the staircase, still putting on his shirt. With his erotic eagerness having quickly run its course, the boy has lost interest in the girl. She hollers hopefully from the room above him, although without following him down the stairs: "Will you call me tomorrow?" He indulges the girl, although with clear ambivalence: "Yeah, sure," he calls back as he leaves via the front door. Feverishly embraced just a few minutes ago, the girl (who has surely been left unsatisfied) has now become for her beau just a needy nag.

With the male lover safely out of the way, the intruder ventures upstairs, snatching a clown mask from the ground and putting it to his face. Eyeholes narrow and thus concentrate our view, almost obscuring bunched-up bedclothes and other evidence of sexual activity upstairs. The intruder scans the room quickly but gives its sexual evidence no real attention. Similarly, despite confronting the now bare-breasted girl, the intruder's gaze does not linger with any absorption on her naked body, which has surely been the fetish-object of the entire scene thus far. She pivots from the mirror, at which she has been brushing her hair, to mark his intrusion—although not with terror but annoyance: "*Michael.*" Michael responds by plunging his knife over and over into her flailing naked form; midway through, his gaze turns with fascination on the knife's raising and falling, the attacker absorbed by the brutality of his own attack. Michael runs down the stairs, panting with exhilaration or nervousness, and straight out of the front door as a car pulls up and two adults, dressed for an evening out, get out and move toward him.

The jig is up when one of them pulls the mask from the intruder's face, again naming him: "Michael!" The scene's first and only cut is used to identify the subject of this thoroughly malevolent first-person perspective as, stunningly, a small boy (Will Sandin). The child stands motionless between his parents, suddenly reinserted into a familial structure and between governing authorities, yet reinserted in a way that only serves to emphasize how irrecoverably that governing structure has just been transgressed. We note that parents have intercepted the child doing something merely weird (rushing outside with a bloodied knife in his hand): they cannot know the full measure of his aberrance. Nor does anyone run inside to obtain the full details; essentially, they act as if they *already* know—that is, they manifest our knowledge and are stunned to silence by its gravity. We note that the suddenly unmasked child—eyes wide, mouth slightly agape—also has no words, no gestures or expressions to frame his outburst: in short, he stands as if he too is surprised to realize that, under that mask, he is just a kid.

This scene is undergirded by a conventional morality that punishes the teenager for her sexuality—a moral schema in which the child (nominally the asexual and domestic subject par excellence) is used as the punishing agent. Subtext aside, we are left oblivious to the child's motive. When Michael returns ten years later (when the rest of the film takes place), we know he murders because he is innately a psycho-killer, a notion that renders the question of motive immaterial and banal. But as a child . . . We might speculate that this killer kid, in the early stages of puberty, lusts after his sister and thus lashes out at her for her promiscuity. Yet with all the scene's voyeuristic peeping and creeping, the

Figure 3.1. After stabbing his sister to death, the six-year-old Michael Myers (Will Sandin) stands mute and stationary between his stunned parents in *Halloween* (John Carpenter, Anchor Bay, 1978). Digital frame enlargement.

sexual motive is in fact the banal one we have been thinking about all along, and the one comprehensively overpowered and rendered trivial by the revelation of the child—a figure staunchly disassociated from sexuality—beneath the mask. In place of sexual jealousy, we have no tangible signifier of motive. The inscrutability of the child's crime is what inflects the scene's final shot, a mystery manifest in the shocked expressions of his parents as well as that of Michael himself. The shot that places this child in the context of adult authority is then accentuated by a traumatically purposeless, gradual zoom-out, receding uncertainly away from its now unclassifiable object. We note that when the startled girl first notices Michael, she reprimands him by name, recognizing him as a child—a recognition that seeks to "belittle" him as such, as in: "Michael, you know better than to be in here." The parent-like authority invoked by this recognition is refused and affronted in a spasm of violence; what imbues this moment with added horror, though, is that despite the girl's serious reproach, the shot absolutely refuses to move from the already established first-person perspective to taking the child as its disempowered object. At the moment of attack, the victim knows and names her attacker. The viewer, however, is still in the dark. Steve Neale describes the cut that identifies the child as "provid[ing] the knowledge desired but frustrated during the span of the opening shot" yet notes that it "undermines any position of relative certainty that may have been reached" because of the killer's anomalous age (358–9). The camera recedes as if, despite Michael's being (finally) stationary, rendered passive and receptive to discipline, he escapes our gaze and our grasp. The child's unpoliced gaze communicates a psychopathy enacted through his very stalking mobility, his roving, autonomous *seeingness*. We have seen a lot and have seen the child seeing way too much. While the child is acknowledged as such with his exposure to the corrective adult gaze, that correction's force is now miniscule and comes way too late.

The pattern of expectation and upheaval enacted here can be elaborated further through exploration of the social significance of Halloween and its relationship to childhood. The scene's trauma references concern for the powerless child, urban legends associated with the holiday such as poisoned or razor blade–infested treats given to trick-or-treaters (nearly nonexistent phenomena treated in detail by Joel Best and Gerald T. Horiuchi), and the increased media observance of incidents of suburban crime during Halloween. Folklorists have identified that urban legends "often depict a clash between modern conditions and some aspect of a traditional lifestyle" (Brunvand 189). Best and Horiuchi elaborate upon this: "In general urban legends are products of social tension or strain" (492). They link the proliferation of urban legends associated with Halloween in the 1960s and 1970s with the promotion of child abuse as a major social problem, a public campaign that implied that "all children were potential victims" (493). Trick or treating, then, is a phenomenon tending to suggest danger to the innocent child from those sadistic adults who, according to folklore, pick Halloween to get busy. In *Halloween*, however, the "trick or treat!" exclamation is used as a perverse precursor to invasion and sadistic murder *by* a child. In fact, it is the teenage girl who is transformed into the innocent here: unself-consciously naked, singing playfully to herself while brushing her hair, and sympathetically overcommitted to the brash sexual partner who surely will not (as she hopefully requests) call her the next day.

We can also consider the scene via further contemplation of trick-or-treat rituals. Gary Cross points out that by the 1940s, "adults were supposed to engage the children by guessing who was behind the mask when they first appeared at the door" (104). In this sense, historically on Halloween the construction of the child as cute and powerless is amplified. Trick-or-treating children are traditionally clothed as figures of threatening power (witches, ghosts, pirates, etc.); beneath the extravagant clothing of uncertainty and terror is the reassuring spectacle of the cute and readily assimilable child, whose part in this ritual thus works to allay social anxiety. However, Cross also indicates that by the mid-1950s, the traditionally frightening crop of ghosts and witches had begun to include more agreeable characters, often from popular children's media (especially Disney productions, 104). It is in this tradition that our child villain is costumed, in his joyous, silken clown clothes. This costume, instead of offering symbols of superstition and dread, gives us first the cutely familiar used to assuage social fears. Beneath that, though, is the horrifyingly empowered and utterly unassimilable.

We look and look for the cutesey kid yet horrifyingly cannot—according to the expected schema—actually find him. This uncertain deferral is surely the haunting effect of the "Trick or treat!" chorus that opens the scene, and that we cannot attach to any children visible onscreen. Murray Pomerance writes that when confronted with unanchored ("acousmatic") sound, "the filmgoer willfully leaps out of his experience to logically map and index the . . . sound within a context that is pragmatic, narratively sensible, and banal" (121); however, the children's voices here and the location from which they flow remain unreconciled. Similarly, the scene's conclusion serves only to indicate our inability to grasp and familiarize this bizarre child. The decentered, unlocated children's voices that begin the film mirror the anomalous, ungraspable child with which we are left. In the slow, nonplussed (even nervous) zoom-out, we find a visual analogue and bookend for the acousmatic sound, which creates, as Pomerance puts it, "a sense of being surrounded by a presence that cannot be identified or grappled with in any way" (113).

Child's-eye–view shots conventionally provoke sentiments of cuteness, uncertainty, and innocence—adjectives that complement adult conceptualizations of the child and uphold the epistemological supremacy of adult perspectives. However, this anomalous viewer scans territory with frighteningly precise and powerful (however inscrutable) intentions. Because of its association with innocence, the child's point of view rarely occurs as more than a naturalized symbol of adult power. "Childish" points of view in popular film may be said to be characterized by their intimate reliance on and silent reference to *adult*, apparently empirical points of view. For example, in a film like *Look Who's Talking* (1989), which combines a baby's point of view with a film's worth of cute and humorous wise-cracks in adult voice-over, we see the adult's idea of what the child sees pushed to its celebratory zenith. While theorists like Gareth Matthews have pointed out that children are indeed capable of what may be genuinely classed as "philosophical thought," in films intended for adult entertainment, "childlike" low-angle shots and cutely canted frames represent a logic of fundamental subordination. Such shots position the child as unavoidably caught up in the gaze of the adult viewer, who invests in them affection, even temporary identification, but not intellectual or epistemological allegiance (see Murray Smith). Thus, the child's point of view does not contradict but upholds the sense of reliability and dominance of adult points of view in that what the child sees lacks substance or focus by comparison with what an adult would see from the same position. Not only does it reflect the hierarchical relationship between adult and child, but it also uses cinema's qualities of visual identification to naturalize it and to provide us with an ideological fiction we do not even identify as such. In this way, maintenance of and complicity in the adult-child hierarchy is not the conscious or moralistic agenda of a narrative, but a condition of our textual access to it.

However, *Halloween* denies the aestheticization of the child and the function of the adult gaze to always already "produce" him through looked-for signifiers of subordination. The final long zoom-out that contextualizes the boy with his parents is ambiguous, slightly off-kilter, withdrawing uncertainly—it does not succeed in returning the child to a "proper" place under the protective aegis of age and wisdom. The vast majority of the opening scene's cinematography charts a first-person subject position; any answering viewpoint (from one of Michael's parents), which might connote a dependable restabilization of the adult gaze, is absent. The sudden shift in perspective serves not only to finally (and coolly) identify the villain, but also to demonstrate how troublingly autonomous his point of view has truly been. While he finally stands as any conventional child might—overseen on either side by Mom and Dad—we cannot recognize him as such. The adults' literal presence as a "frame" for this disturbing viewpoint serves only to emphasize how far away we are (and they with us) and how automatically and powerfully we expect what we imagine the child sees to be its reality.

## The To-Be-Looked-At Child

In her essay "Visual Pleasure and Narrative Cinema" (1975), Laura Mulvey examined the way the cinema had historically designated a masculine subject position for the audience by positioning women as objects of visual pleasure and mastery for men. Mulvey's critique proceeds from the idea that cinema offers certain types of pleasure, one of which is scopophilia, the pleasure of "looking" (8), and she draws upon Jacques Lacan's work pointing to the gaze as a visual "motive" that implicitly accepts and arranges the positioning of subjects in society with reference to one another and, specifically, according to sexual difference. For Lacan, the heterosexual relationship is always structured around the phallic signifier, a totemic masculinity against which the feminine subject perceives her own inadequacy. When gazing at a woman, a male presumes (or "looks for") signification of *lack*.[2] Mulvey's enduring critique suggests that traditionally the woman onscreen is positioned within this field for the (male) viewer, encouraging him to acknowledge her lack and confirming his empowered possession. According to Mulvey, in classical Hollywood cinema, not only are viewers encouraged to identify with male protagonists, but women are positioned in a way that implies voyeuristic male pleasure, rendering them already-coded objects of male desire. While Mulvey's essay failed to address the pleasure taken by female viewers or the possibility of more diverse modes of viewing generally, it remains of interest in its illustration of the way cultural (in this case patriarchal) dominance is expressed or amplified through spectatorship, its understanding of how films, as cultural products, "[reinforce] pre-existing patterns of fascination already at work within the individual subject and the social formations that have moulded him" (6). The emphasis Mulvey places on the power inherent in spectatorship, its ability to designate passivity and activity through cultural expectation, is acutely relevant to the depiction and perception of adult-child power relations in film. While the "motive" of the gaze might differ in this case, the passive/active dynamic Mulvey observes has much in common with the relationship of the onscreen child to the viewer and adult protagonist, thus indicating its usefulness for contemplating horror's physically small but very nasty starers.

In films intended for adult audiences, the child is always imbued with what Mulvey refers to as a predefining *to-be-looked-at-ness*, visually subordinated according to the adult-child power hierarchy, through which his vulnerability is romanticized. The particular prevalence of this way of seeing cinematic children is indicated by the exaggeratedly "cute" children in films such as *Village of the Damned* or *The Bad Seed* (1956), whose presentation is clearly associated with an adult pleasure through looking. After the fashion of Shirley Temple or other "adorable" child stars, the children's appearance draws upon a series of stylized visual cues that respond to and stimulate a predetermining adult gaze. In other words, these children are dressed to impress. The pleasurable recognition of the cute or innocent child through looking, like Mulvey's *to-be-looked-at-ness*, contains the unconscious assumption that control will be affirmed and consolidated through spectatorship. The appreciation of cuteness confirms the child's passivity: he is seen as open to our conceptualizations. In Lori Merish's words, it "aestheticizes powerlessness" (187). This *to-be-looked-at-ness* is most obvious in those films whose priorities include visually delighting us with the innocent and adorable child. To pick a much-celebrated example, in *Jerry Maguire* (1996) we meet the blond and cutely bespectacled Ray Boyd (Jonathan Lipnicki), the five-year-old son of Dorothy Boyd (Renée Zellweger), the titular protagonist's love interest and employee. Ray performs for our admiring gaze, speaking in cutely goofy nonsequiturs ("Let's go to the zoo!"), and sweetly answering the phone to Jerry's prized and precious client (Cuba Gooding Jr.), thus comically juxtaposing his joyful young self with the stress of adult affairs.

In this particular example, the child pleases our adult gaze in a sustained, noticeable, and celebrated way, yet this *to-be-looked-at-ness* is always somehow referenced in representations of children onscreen. Looking is the means by which we recognize subjects according to visual and cultural codes and alleviate the distances between selves and Others. The child is conceived as an Other, but one who must be regulated according to a given set of cultural norms: he or she is seen as the object of a dominating cultural discourse and visually interpreted as ideologically complacent. In viewing the child, however he or she looks and whatever he or she is doing, the adult frames this child's appearance and behavior with reference to a culturally desired (passive) child. Whereas a hostile adult may be viewed as representing ideological opposition—as threateningly suggesting another point of view—even the child's most violent tantrum can be accommodated by culturally comprehensible paradigms that presuppose children are "controllable" or "in need of control." These paradigms code children as "bad" or "good," judgments whose reference is the paradigmatic (adult) activity of parenting and its ideal outcome of an already imagined, sweetly obedient child. That is, through the adult gaze and its expectation of children's passivity, the child's behavior is neatly confined within the sphere we know as "childhood." Because of the power wrapped up in the way we look at the child, in what we expect to see when we do it, the superficially unremarkable spectacle of the staring child assumes explosive (and, for the adult, damning) significance. The staring child is a figure who not only rejects the "childish" (passive) position prescribed for it but also powerfully refutes the entire adult-child hierarchy.

## Eyes That Paralyze: *Village of the Damned*

The children of Wolf Rilla's *Village of the Damned* are exemplarily nefarious starers: their eyes glow relentlessly as they direct their victims to gruesome (and often spectacular) acts of self-harm. After Midwich village is overcome by a mysterious intergalactic force that has, without warning, rendered every inhabitant unconscious and left every female of childbearing age pregnant, the communal slumber leads to the birth of terrifying children whose telepathic ability is signified and enacted by their hypnotic eyes. The children's origin means that their monstrousness (unlike that of the child in *Halloween*) is also obscurely connected with the extraterrestrial. In this film, and in Carpenter's 1995 remake, the use of staring children as representations of this draws its power from the tension generated by children's refusal to reciprocate dominant adult perspectives of them. The *Village of the Damned* films begin by designating for the viewer a specifically adult position of spectatorship and through this (at least initially) promote the *to-be-looked-at-ness* of children in support of that position. The children's glowing eyes and persistent stare, however, serve as unsettling signifiers that the way in which adults interpret them visually is not objective, as is so confidently assumed: these children have an interpretive program of their own.

From outset to conclusion, the audience is invited to identify only with the adult protagonists in *Village of the Damned*. The adult goal of rational coexistence and nonviolence is transparent and sensibly articulated, whereas the children's origin, nature, and intentions are impenetrably mystified. Professor Zellaby (George Sanders) is our primary representative: a rational authority on whom we can lean, eschewing the hotheaded outbursts of peripheral characters who would do away with the children without compunction and gathering clues for the viewer as to their nature. The children are only destroyed once the Professor decides that it is appropriate. Although Midwich contains other, normal children, they assume no role as characters with whom viewers might identify. A scene in which one of the Dayout children is given a puzzle—a treat concealed within a small wooden box composed of a network of sliding compartments—might appear to align the viewer with a child, but in fact it reinforces the film's adult-centric perspective. As Zellaby hands the contraption to the Dayout child, an infant held in his mother's (Jenny

Figure 3.2. Beware the stare: the children of *Village of the Damned* (Rilla, Warner Bros., 1960) exercise their hypnotic gaze. Digital frame enlargement.

Laird's) arms, it is snatched away by his normal, older male sibling in a typical moment of brotherly bullying. The brother's clumsy and fundamentally childlike attempts to solve the puzzle himself are interrupted by his younger and stranger sibling, who transfixes him with his glowing gaze, much to the surrounding adults' intrigue. The ensuing shots appear to approximate the stared-at boy's perspective, subjecting us to the same hypnotic sight; however, despite the command the infant now exerts over the boy, the shot resists subjecting us to any more than a medium close-up that keeps the contextualizing visual reminder of the mother's body, thus compromising our full immersion. An "objective" adult position of spectatorship is thus irrepressibly present when the mother's face curiously turns to focus on the staring child she holds in her arms. The intrusion of the mother's line of sight ensures the encounter remains a spectacle rather than a subjective sensation, maintaining a steady reminder of the presence of adult observers. The adults present—Zellaby; his military brother-in-law, Alan (Michael Gwynn); and the children's mother—then silently trade glances, a conversation of looks that excludes children's perspectives, reinforcing an elevated logic of adult observation in which children are objectified. The adults' exchange of amazed looks, each acknowledging the other's spectatorship, repeatedly reconfirms the adult viewing position and fortifies the viewer's affective identification with the film's adult characters.

The stability of this perspective is key to contextualizing the hostility of the child's gaze. In films such as *Village of the Damned*, the supposition of an adult viewer constructs the child with reference to specifically adult modes of seeing. Lori Merish's discussion of "the cute" is of particular use here. For Merish, the appreciation of children as cute "romanticizes the child's dependency on social or familial environments; a child is cute insofar as it can be considered "part of the 'family,' indeed part of the self" (187). When we look at the child, we do so with this visual program in mind, drawing the child into what Merish calls a "drama of socialization" that seeks to locate it within accepted cultural norms. The appreciation of cuteness is indicative of elevated perception, a narcissistic looking for characteristics to which the spectator can attach meaning. In turn, cuteness constructs its subjects as powerless and willing to be constructed. Appreciation of the cute depicts the cute child as passive and reliant, particularly on the empowered (adult) spectator: "What the cute stages is, in part, a need for adult care" (Merish 187). In this way, cuteness connotes not only vulnerability and reliance but also total passivity to surrounding (adult) culture. The appearance of the children in *Village of the Damned* clearly signals an appeal to stereotypical Western (and white supremacist) constructions of cuteness: tidy appearance, blond hair, fair skin. These attributes are part of a *to-be-looked-at* spectacle of childhood that supports adult control. Carpenter's 1995 remake commences by promoting adult visual pleasure through the spectacle of a school fair. The initial narrative focus is on the organization of the event and thereby demarcates an adult epistemological domain that lovingly oversees a spectacle of childish innocence. These scenes fetishize the cuteness and vulnerability of the child by emphasizing adult responsibility and pleasure in doing things for children. A more concentrated example of the child's *to-be-looked-at-ness* comes to the fore in this film as Dayout child David (Thomas Dekker) dresses himself before a large mirror. To the accompaniment of a quiet, wistful score, the reflection in the mirror constructs the child as adorably tender (thus malleable), and the pleasure offered by his appearance is confirmed when we see the boy's mother (Linda Kozlowski) watching him from the doorway. However, the mother's attempt to indulge the boy's cuteness by brushing his hair is refused. As he leaves the mirror he tells her, "I'm old enough to do things by myself": a denial of the translation of cuteness into the dependence and adult control it seemingly emblematizes.

It is because of the power tied up with how children are looked at that the child's stare is such a forceful motif of villainy in Rilla's and Carpenter's films. Both *Village of the Damned* films encourage the viewer to take a specifically adult pleasure in viewing the child characters, thereby implicitly consolidating the assumptions of that pleasure: control over and epistemological dominance of children. The disruptive potential of the looking child stems from its challenge to adult dominance outwardly signified by the child's appearance and its (adult) interpretation. In Rilla's original, the children's eyes glow white as they attack, and they glow anything from orange to green in Carpenter's color remake. This display stuns the children's victims speechless, rendering them unable to move before forcing them to perform some grisly act of suicide. The staring draws alarming attention to the child as *spectator*, overturning the control presumed by the adult gaze.

Carpenter's film contains a number of moments that further indicate the power invested in positions of spectatorship: when the father of one of the Dayout children (Peter Jason) very nearly runs over Dayout ringleader Mara (Lindsey Haun) in his car, he rushes to her aid, bending down to occupy the same frame in a posture that implies her vulnerability. Reverse cutting between the two provides an example of cinematic angles betraying the ideology of adult-child relations: the man crouches down to ensure the girl's safety, assuming a condescending imitation of her point of view. However, his sense of dominance is disrupted when the girl (who is neither injured nor troubled by the fact that she might have been) willfully denies him information about his missing daughter. As his temper changes, so too does his height: he raises himself back to adult proportions, seeking to reinforce Mara's vulnerability through a reminder of his elevated adult gaze and thus his authority.

The Dayout children's confrontation with their school's alcoholic, child-hating janitor (George Flower) also indicates that their villainy is wrapped up in their denial of the empiricism of adult perspectives: their willingness to look *back*. Entering their classroom in the teacher's absence, the janitor proceeds to admonish the children for the town's misfortunes. The switch to the children's point of view signaled by a low-angle pan of the man pacing back and forth presents the adult as paradoxically powerless before his seemingly diminutive spectators (a suggestion confirmed by a number of quick cuts to close-ups of the children, who, despite the man's raving, are clearly unworried). The brutish stress of the janitor's remark to one of these children (Cody Dorkin), "I don't like the way you're lookin' at me, boy," demonstrates his attempt to restore his own diminished visual power. The janitor laments that since the children arrived, he has been left "watchin' people leave this town, watchin' things die," and we again infer the children's hostile confinement of adults to the role of impotent gazers. After the janitor accidentally wallops the same beady-eyed boy across the head with the handle of his broom, the point of view switches to the janitor's high-angle perspective as the affected child, along with his equally morose buddies, stands up from his desk and stares back even more intensely. The boy's bold gesture rejects the adult predefinition of the child, and the janitor's attempt to stare him down (to passivity). "Well, ain't you gonna to do something!" the janitor barks, affronted by the children's refusal to display their vulnerability before him: "Aren't ya gonna bawl like all the other piss ants?" Instead, the boy's eyes, along with those of his cohorts, glow brilliant green, guiding the hypnotized man to a rooftop where, still under the children's direction, he commits suicide. As in the opening scene of *Halloween*, the temporary adoption of a child's point of view serves to belittle the authority of the usually superior adult gaze. Here, however, a challenge to the adult way of looking is amplified into an agent of literal violence.

Carol J. Clover casts doubt on the notion that point of view in film necessarily equals what we can properly call "identification," writing that "the fact that Steven Spielberg can stage an attack in *Jaws* from the shark's point of view . . . or Hitchcock an attack in *The Birds* from the bird's-eye perspective . . . would seem to suggest either that the viewer's identificatory powers are unbelievably elastic or that point-of-view shots can sometimes be pro forma" (208). Such shots from a villain's or aggressor's perspective are a convention of horror that communicates a momentary sense of the powerlessness of the viewer/protagonist. The use of infrared alien vision in *Predator* (1987) suggests the vulnerability of a group of muscular Special Forces troops hunted by the blood-thirsty extraterrestrial—the viewer identifies with the men rather than the creature and recognizes the perspective shift as a nervous revocation of control. In the staring child we see a similar invalidation of control. As a symbol of villainy, the child's eyes bring out the immense ideological investment in adult modes of viewing children, preying on both the epistemological prioritization of adult characters and attitudes and our ability to be lured by children's cute and thus apparently powerless presentation. Even in those horror films that might appear to adopt the child's perspective by having powerful children as protagonists, such as *Firestarter* (1984) and *The Shining* (1980), the child is always framed by adult agendas of control, behaving, in the end, as the adult wishes him or her to. In *Firestarter*, employees of a mysterious government facility called "The Shop" attempt to capture a girl named Charlene (Drew Barrymore) who has the ability to tell the near future and to set objects on fire through mental exertion. The government employees are villains in this film precisely because they are interested in taking away from the child her natural right to "be a child"—her ability not only to lead a normal life but to fulfill the role outlined for her by adults. Charlene's condition is treated as a medical ailment that needs to be controlled by adults, and she cries when her powers are used without her father's consent. Ultimately, the child's seemingly autonomous power is used to validate and clarify adult agendas of control. At the film's conclusion, she burns to death the agent who seeks to capture her (George C. Scott) and who, in doing so, threatens to usurp her father's authority. Essentially, the child's power over adults is subordinate to the power adults have over her. "Deep down," writes Kathy Merlock Jackson, "she remains innocent" (153). The flight-of-the-innocent focus of films like *Firestarter* and *The Shining*, in which child heroes are pitted against adult aggressors, does not represent their child protagonists as truly active subjects: they are already contained by adult perspectives of the child's proper place and, ultimately, the necessary safeguarding of the hierarchical relationship between adult and child. These films encourage and affirm the viewer's expectation of the *to-be-looked-at* child, and do not ultimately challenge the dominance of the adult gaze. Yet the children of horror film do not look so "childishly" or "innocently"; the meaning of their first-person perspectives, and of the eyes that signify them, is horrifyingly ambiguous.

## Conclusion

Viewers and protagonists alike are perfectly aware that children have the ability to see. It is the way that understandings of children are supported through the act of seeing, and of their being seen seeing, that creates tension around the perspectives of child villains in *Halloween* and the *Village of the Damned* films as well as others that play with this motif. The child's eyes serve the constant purpose of alerting the viewer to him or her as an active, *looking* subject, upsetting the power of the adult gaze and underscoring the falseness of its claim to universality. It is of course the very strength of the literalization of the innocent child in film, the pervasiveness of this cultural characterization, that allows the child villain's gaze to assume such supreme, destructive, and enduring force. Deeply intertwined with the idea of the idealized, innocent child is our assumption that that child is unable or unwilling to employ his or her gaze as a force of domination—unwilling to look back. The actual physical violence attributed to the stare in a film like *Village of the Damned* illustrates the paranoiac, cultural intolerability of an active child subject, the lurking "demon force" of the unmapped gaze.

# 4

## "The Hand That Rocks the Cradle"

### The Child Villain's Malignant Mom

T HE FATHERS OF VILLAINOUS children are traditionally a busy bunch. The daddy dearest of the original bad seed, Rhoda Penmark (Patty McCormack), is dragged out the front door on military duty within the film's first five minutes; the yuppie dad of the eponymous problem child in *Joshua* (2007) is dealing with a stock market upheaval; the father of Mark (Elijah Wood) in *The Good Son* (1993), despite the tragic loss of his wife, is forced to fly to the other side of the world on business, leaving his son to contend with psycho cousin Henry (Macaulay Culkin) and his blindly devoted mother. In films featuring terrible children, everyone knows where the father is: he is at work—it is the mother who is left to account for the child's waywardness. Critics such as Kathy Merlock Jackson and William Paul have noted that the father's absence is a common feature of films such as *The Exorcist* (1973) and *The Bad Seed* (1956), implying that the mother, from these films' perspectives, cannot be depended on to keep the family unit functional. Several of these films are marked by consternation and dread over the changing nature of motherhood and the power of mothers as domestic carers, subtly rooting the child's villainy in her mother's character. Contemplating *The Exorcist*, Barbara Creed writes, "What better ground for the forces of evil to take root than the household of a family in which the father is absent and where the mother continually utters profanities, particularly in relation to her husband?" (34). On the one hand, the mother's traditional closeness to the child seems to afford her unique—potentially nefarious—power over her offspring; on the other hand, any failure or refusal by her to perform the requirements of her traditional role is seen to produce a child wide open to corruption.

Several child villain films demonstrate deep uncertainty around the irrepressibly bodily, irrepressibly maternal acts of birth and physical nurture; in addition, they fret over the apparent totality of women's control of the domestic sphere. After all, "[t]he hand that rocks the cradle," proclaims the famous William Ross Wallace poem, "is the hand that rules the world." The first clause, of course, was also the title of a successful 1992 thriller starring Rebecca De Mornay (the second clause forming the ready-made tagline)—a film whose vision of maternal power grimly rearticulated Wallace's (originally ecstatic) lines in the popular imagination. Curtis Hanson's *The Hand That Rocks the Cradle* does not feature a child villain, yet its anxious dramatization of the mother-child bond makes it an interesting place to begin contemplating many films that do.

When pregnant Claire Bartel (Annabella Sciorra) visits sleazy gynecologist Victor Mott (John de Lancie), he insists on performing a perhaps more than usually thorough examination. Our suspicions of him are confirmed when, having parted Claire's legs, he slides off his latex medical glove in order to more fully experience his analysis. Claire huffs and pivots her head from side to side, discomforted but (we assume) still unaware that this examination is more sensory than analytical. However, Mott's villainy is announced unambiguously when, having slid into a momentary erotic trance, he begins simultaneously massaging Claire's pregnant stomach. Claire storms out in distress, then timorously files a complaint, only to have her reluctant voice strengthened by a throng of similar grievances from other patients. Knowing his career is done for (something that counts for much in the white-collar world of the film), the doctor bites the bullet (literally), leaving behind his distinctly pregnant wife (De Mornay). Mrs. Mott is soon informed that her husband's assets will be frozen by the state in anticipation of a substantial legal payout to his victims and that his suicide means she won't see a penny from his insurance company. Knowing that the lifestyle of dependence and luxury to which she has grown accustomed is at an ignominious end, Mrs. Mott collapses and loses her child as a result of the fall. Newly destitute and by now very irate, she assumes the persona of "Peyton Flanders" and secures a position as the Bartel family nanny, a vantage point from which she proceeds to short circuit the Bartels' life of bourgeois bliss.

*The Hand That Rocks the Cradle's* defining image of invasion comes when Peyton creeps up to the room of baby Joe Bartel, pillow poised. Instead of vengefully smothering the infant, however, she props the pillow behind his head, unbuttons her gown, and proceeds to breastfeed him, an act she continues secretly throughout the film. The nefarious nanny is discovered and gorily dispatched by film's end, tumbling from a roof and catching a piece of fence paling through the abdomen on the way down in a brutal reminder of her crimes against motherhood. Through its depiction of subversive nurture, however, the film hypothesizes a child villain as its narrative climax: the ingestion of the product of another woman's body will somehow contaminate and diffuse the infant's connection to its mother. Prior to Peyton's death, Bartel family friend and real estate go-getter Marlene Craven (Julianne Moore) quotes the film's title to Claire as a piece of corporate wisdom against letting another woman "take up a power-position in your home." Marlene's advice is followed by an immediate cutaway of Peyton, again insidiously suckling the Bartel babe in the family's home. Of course, the spectacle presented here is ostensibly straightforward—banal, even—yet the film constructs it as a ritual of preternatural power: a formerly innocent tot is now a child villain in the making.

The focus of *The Hand That Rocks the Cradle* on the mother figure as physical caregiver and stable foundation of domesticity makes explicit the power attributed to mothering in horror films featuring more overt child villains. The film's investment in breastfeeding, particularly, suggests that fears of motherhood's power are rooted in male feelings of illegitimacy alongside women's more overtly biological connection to their children as well as a lack of confidence in mothers to adequately secure their "exclusive" domain. *The Hand That Rocks the Cradle* is deeply informed by a culture suspicious of the contemporary multifariousness of "motherhood." In response to her desire to build a greenhouse, for example, Claire's husband instructs her that she cannot hope "to do everything." The bustling businesswoman Marlene articulates this notion with a more rhetorical twang when she laments that "these days a woman can feel like a failure if she doesn't bring in fifty grand a year and still make time for blowjobs and homemade lasagna." It is a line that echoes the spirit, if not the analytical inclination, of E. Ann Kaplan's 1990 essay "Sex, Work and Motherhood: The Impossible Triangle," which discusses "the lack of facilitating institutions" (409) for women hoping to combine the three. The politics of this problem are, however, forcefully overwritten by the narrative's immediate worry that the motherhood idealized by liberal patriarchy, far from having its house in order, has left our children vulnerable to corruption.

*The Hand That Rocks the Cradle* exists on a continuum with a tradition of evil child films imbued with fears over women's "privileged" position in relation to their offspring and their changing roles in society. Conventionally, as Kaplan suggests elsewhere, motherhood may have "been repressed on all levels except that of hypostatization, romanticization, and idealization" (*Women and Film* 201). However, the topsy-turvy territory of horror has consistently laid our anxieties bare, constructing mothers' relationship to their children as one of both fearsome power and reprehensible incompetence.

## Treachery on the Home Front

That landmark of child villainy, *The Bad Seed*, was produced at the height of the Cold War, just two months prior to Khrushchev's thunderous assurance to Western delegates that "[w]e will bury you" ("We Will Bury You," *Time*). The first "fear" invoked in the film, as Cyndy Hendershot points out, is that of nuclear war (6), when Rhoda Penmark's (Patty McCormack's) father, Colonel Penmark (William Hopper), is whisked away to fulfill his patriotic duty. What is remarkable is the confident treatment of that threat, the deflection of anxiety onto the state of the family home during times of paternal absence, and the consequent reconstruction of the domestic sphere as the real zone of fallout. In *The Bad Seed* we see not merely a decontextualized demonization of the child, but also a powerful skepticism of motherhood brought on by the changing roles of women during the war years. It is this skepticism of motherhood—a skepticism that reemerges in a number of later child villain films—that this brief third discussion of *The Bad Seed* centralizes. However subtly, the film pins part of the blame for Rhoda's transgressions on her mother (Nancy Kelly), critiquing her efficacy as an authority figure while spitefully caricaturing contemporary motherhood through landlady Monica Breedlove (Evelyn Varden), a banal yet potent corrupter of the domesticity left behind by the Colonel.

Colonel Penmark is the blond-haired American good guy who painfully (but rightly, from the film's point of view) puts his country first. As he leaves, he assures his wife that they've "lived through this before": the film gives us no reason to believe that this sturdy soldier isn't up to the job. Christine, however, is overcome by a romantic attachment that smacks of selfishness under the circumstances: "Oh Kenneth," she groans. Attempting to soothe his wife's anxiety, the Colonel looks into her eyes with a cozy query that cues a familiar response: "My girl?" he asks. "For ever and ever," she responds. The exchange, clearly rehearsed previously—some self-consciously romantic routine the two act out—not only implies Christine's reliance on the Colonel but also reminds us of the man's similarly rhetorical exchange with his daughter prior to saying goodbye: "What'll you give me for a basket of kisses?" he asks; "I'll give you a basket of hugs!" comes the response. In her similarly too-girly goodbye, the film establishes Christine's own infantilism, a childlike reliance on male authority that implies parental inadequacy and aligns her with the soon-to-be recalcitrant Rhoda. The ambivalence with which Christine embraces *her* duty within the domestic sphere is expressed spatially as she dawdles on the pavement outside after her husband has left. As the Colonel's car rolls away, the score is overcome by a deep woodwind grumble that forcefully signals the instability of the domestic environment triggered by his absence.

Michael Rogin's discussion of Cold War–era cinema directs attention to the increased public scrutiny of mothers and their prescribed role within the family home throughout the 1940s and 1950s. This was particularly manifest in disdain for what became known as "momism," after the target of Philip Wylie's 1942 book of social criticism *A Generation of Vipers*. Rogin explains that momism centered on what Wylie saw as

> a self righteous, hypocritical, sexually repressed, middle-aged woman. Having lost the household functions of preindustrial women, according to Wylie, mom got men to worship her and spend money on her instead. . . . Mom dominated her husband and encouraged the dependence of her son. (6)

In the form of the vociferous landlady and Penmark family friend Monica, this characterization looms larger over *The Bad Seed* than any nuclear disaster. A loud, self-serving busybody, she barges into the film's opening scene, disrupting the father's farewell. "No life of my own so I lead other people's," she boasts, holding the floor while helping herself to a container of chocolates on a nearby table. Breedlove is certainly a send-up of the egotistical indulgence allegedly pursued by wartime women, her attention-seeking presence subtly belittling the Colonel's sacrifice as he leaves the family he adores behind. Through Christine and Breedlove, *The Bad Seed* effectively separates motherhood into two figures: Breedlove personifies the increasing intrusion of "momism" into the domestic sphere, whereas Christine demonstrates the moral and authoritative failure of the traditional mother to overcome it.

Christine leaves Rhoda in Monica's company as she sees to her departing husband, although when she reenters the home, things have already taken a turn for the worse: Rhoda is modeling a pair of rhine-

Figure 4.1. Dark delights: Monica Breedlove (Evelyn Varden) initiates Rhoda Penmark (Patty McCormack) into the pleasures of consumerism in *The Bad Seed* (Mervyn LeRoy, Warner Bros., 1956). Digital frame enlargement.

stone-studded sunglasses given to her by Monica, their lenses darkly illustrating the pleasures of materialism.

Monica, rather than Christine, is reflected in the mirror behind the girl, standing over her with a Mephistophelian grin: an arrangement indicative of a reflective relationship between the two. The swooping shadow of an airplane statuette on a table nearby helps fuse wartime instability with this spectacle of female consumerism and invokes the absent father as the third member of this newly "familial" triad. The sudden cut back to Christine confirms her as a startled and excluded witness to corruption: "Didn't you ever hear about spoiling people?" she chides Breedlove.

*The Bad Seed*'s primary emotional dilemma puts Christine's devotion to her daughter in direct competition with her moral duty to turn her in. In this respect, as a caring mother racked with guilt over her daughter's abominable crimes, Christine undoubtedly courts the viewer's sympathy. Rogin points out that in the 1950s, the virtues of traditional maternal domesticity couldn't be emphasized enough: "mothers were sanctified, not vilified" (7). However, in light of contemporary anxiety over women's employment outside the family home (and over juvenile delinquency, with which it was associated), it was praise embedded with complaint. *The Bad Seed* deploys the intrusive Breedlove not only as a derisive caricature of recent female economic liberation during the war years but also as a demonstration of the child's vulnerability to the corrupting influences of that Othered mother. When, later in the film, a radio report communicates that a child has been killed during the school picnic, Breedlove assures Christine that it simply could not have been Rhoda, who is "far too self-reliant a child," vociferously recognizing her own characteristics in the pushy little materialist she feels she has bred. Also befitting fears surrounding women in the war years, Breedlove's interest in psychoanalysis is phrased to suggest sexual promiscuity. She gleefully chimes that psychoanalysis helped her end her marriage, and her brother's quip that "Monica's been spread out on couches from New York to Los Angeles" earns him a punishing stare. The film introduces psychoanalysis ostensibly as a pretext for Christine to dredge up the repressed memory of being adopted; however, her Oedipal fondness for her father allows Freud's schema to generally amplify concern over women's potentially wayward sexuality. While he is off on duty, Mr. Penmark thoughtfully posts presents back to his daughter (a tea set, symbolic of his civility), this ensuring we know where his thoughts and affections are anchored. Yet at home, his wife is not merely indulging in fantasies about other men—but thinking about her own father!

Drawing upon the work of Georges Bataille, Hendershot interprets *The Bad Seed*, along with *The Fly* (1958) and *Psycho* (1960), as pointing toward a Cold War preoccupation with taboo and transgression: "Rhoda's transgressions seem to mirror the transgressions of a Cold War military with its plans for nuclear war and very real radiation experiments on human subjects" (26). Although this broad reading is helpful in emphasizing the awareness of cultural transgression in a United States supposedly brimming with communists, it is important to note the film's emphasis of maternal rather than military upheaval in its depiction of Rhoda's descent into criminality. Breedlove operates in tandem with Christine to establish the image of a home bereft of stable authority. The ineptitude with which Christine handles her antagonistic imp and allows Breedlove to intrude on her domestic duty in the Colonel's absence exemplifies the contemporary skepticism of motherhood. In the brief time he is onscreen, the Colonel even manages to demonstrate what an adequate parent he is, censoring himself in Rhoda's presence ("You said 'by *gum*' because I was here, didn't you?"). Christine meanwhile acts out her own childishness and inability to seize control of the domestic sphere, leaving it prey to the freewheeling materialism of Breedlove. What is of course omitted in this account—in its implication of blame—is that Christine's immaturity is fostered and fetishized by the Colonel, whose affections routinely infantilize her in accordance with the sexist and patriarchal culture of the time.

The genetic thesis expounded by *The Bad Seed*'s narrative would have us believe that Rhoda's evil stems from a taint in the mother's lineage. As I noted earlier, we finally learn in the film that Christine was adopted: her real mother is killer nurse Bessie Denker, who did away with nine of her patients for their life insurance. The revelation of this lineage appears to absolve Christine and Breedlove of fault (that is, Rhoda's genes are the problem, not her spoiled upbringing). However, Denker's crimes are socially coded, her murders driven by monetary motives that evoke a stereotyped association of women with material goods and (through her occupation as nurse) enacted via the treacherous inversion of an idealized, nurturing maternity. A debased maternity and female materialism are thus not separate from Rhoda's demonism, but are deeply embedded within it. Moreover, this "inherent" materialism is socially reflected for good measure. Breedlove detects nothing sinister in the girl's desires because they so clearly resemble her own. Eventually, the long-suffering mother attempts to do away with her deadly daughter with a meal of sleeping pills and take her own life with a gunshot. Although both survive (in Rhoda's case, only to be struck dead by lightning shortly thereafter), the murder-suicide plot signifies not only the painful connection Christine shares with her child (that she cannot bear to turn her in) but also her internalized sense of fault. That is, Christine's suicide attempt is not merely a response to Rhoda's transgressions, but also Christine's answer to feelings of her own aberrance.

## Sons of Bitches: *The Brood*

Whereas *The Hand That Rocks the Cradle* and *The Bad Seed* bear the scorch marks of cultural climates associated with the changing sociopolitical roles of women, David Cronenberg's 1979 bloodcurdler *The Brood* lays specific emphasis on anxieties of paternal control in light of the mother's reproductive power. Here, the mother's biological closeness to the child is presented as an unassailable affront to male parentage. Her proximity is transformed into a paranoid fantasy in which children become grotesque automatons of maternal power. Perhaps the most diabolical (and certainly the most nauseating) rendering of mother-child might, *The Brood* concerns a horde of snarling mutant tots who enact the violent, unconscious desires of their snarling matriarch, Nola (Samantha Eggar). Art Hinkle plays the film's emotional center, nice-guy husband Frank Carveth, whose wife's institutionalization leaves him as the sole caregiver for their eight-year-old daughter, Candice (Cindy Hinds). While bathing

Candice, Frank is horrified by her bruised body, presumably the result of her time spent with Nola, who is working through trauma left over from childhood abuse inflicted by her own mother. Furious and fearing for his child's safety, Frank arranges to deprive the reclusive woman of access to Candice. He is met with opposition from Nola's therapist, suave psychiatric guru Hal Raglan (Oliver Reed). Raglan is the pioneer of a controversial new discipline called "psychoplasmics," a therapeutic role-playing technique in which the patient's emotional upheaval is brought literally to the surface, breaking out in the form of skin boils and lesions. As Frank follows up his legal options, a mystery intruder in a child's snowsuit savagely murders Nola's alcoholic mother (Nuala Fitzgerald). Later, while visiting the abandoned house where his ex-wife was killed, Nola's father (Harry Beckman) is also killed, caught off guard as he drunkenly bemoans his relationship with his estranged wife. Frank eventually confronts the attacker: while appearing superficially childlike, the creature is revealed as a hideous albino atrocity, another two of which abduct Candice from her school. The film's shock conclusion reveals that Nola is the literal mother of the grotesque "brood": psychoplasmic products of her suppressed rage. In the film's final scene, she elevates her nightgown to reveal a grisly extrauterine sac attached to her abdomen—duly stunning Frank, who has come to Candice's rescue.

Figure 4.2. Monstrous fecundity: Nola (Samantha Eggar) reveals the obscene birthing apparatus from which child monsters emerge in David Cronenberg's *The Brood* (Canadian Film Development Corporation, 1979). Digital frame enlargement.

Nola tears open the bulbous outgrowth to remove a newborn addition to the beastly batch from a goopy mess of blood and membrane. Horror-struck, Frank nevertheless manages to rescue Candice before the brood get to her and throttles to death their psychic mastermind, Nola.

The divorce rate in Cronenberg's native Canada rose by more than 200 percent in the period from 1970 to 1980, soaring to its highest ever in 1987 (*Statistics Canada*), and *The Brood* is thoroughly undergirded by a culture of separation and family instability, a subject that by his own admission affected the director and the film's representative landscape (Creed 44). For Richard Scheib, "[t]here's a real anger and bitterness that propels the film as Cronenberg metaphorizes his divorce, spiraling down into a dark subtext of custody battles and bitter resentment." The battle over Candice, waged from the mother's side with an acidity that eclipses both rationality and Candice's own desires, certainly speaks to Scheib's assertion. *The Brood* is populated with divorced and estranged spouses; Frank's attempt to kindle a relationship with Candice's schoolteacher is sabotaged by a phone call from his wife in a scenario that clearly indicates the film's underlying theme of marital breakdown. "The film allegorizes personal drama," writes William Beard, "and carries a recognizable private conflict, domestic and generational, into the amplified metaphorical conventions of the horror genre" (32). What we see in *The Brood* is both a fearsome dramatization of postmarital antipathy and a paranoiac vision of maternal control over the child.

In *The Brood*, there is no sustained attempt to engage with the flawed female's perspective. As bluntly wholesome as his name suggests, Frank is prominently positioned as the viewer's surrogate, and the film gives us no reason to question his frustration with his estranged wife and his desire to remove Candice from her volatile orbit. Early in the film, Frank's discovery of his daughter's bruises positions us as not only parental but "fatherly," foregrounding the child's need for physical protection. However, his intentions to protect her are hindered when his lawyer candidly informs him that despite what is fair or what isn't, "the law believes in motherhood." Alternatively, Nola's own devotion to Candice is nothing but narcissistic. For her, control of the child is paramount: she admits that she would rather kill Candice than surrender her to Frank. In the hurried cadences of mental fragility, she raves, "[Frank] thinks that I'm trying to make Candy into baby Nola." "Is he right?" the psychiatrist penetratingly questions.

This, of course, is also what the brood are: "Like zombies," writes Barbara Creed, "without a mind of their own they are completely at their mother's bidding. They are, in fact, the mother" (45). The creatures' angrily pinched, catlike countenances evoke Nola as witch and the mutants as her familiars (indeed, the extra nipplelike growths on her torso indicate that the creatures may literally suckle from her body). The naturally brief life span of the mutants represents both their status as physical manifestations of temporary, extreme emotions and their unsustainable freakishness as "monstrous births." These children are abominations—illegitimate attempts at autonomous reproduction doomed by the laws of nature. Bleached albino features suggest their abortive, "unfinished" nature: they are idiot human canvases bereft of the characterizing "essence" apparently bestowed by the male in the reproductive process. Their muteness indicates their inherent lack of reason, constructing them as purely physical expressions of psychic upheaval. As Creed points out, "[p]arthenogenesis is impossible, but if it could happen, the film seems to be arguing, woman could give birth only to deformed manifestations of herself" (47).

Creed seizes upon *The Brood*'s "feminine" grotesque to read the film primarily in terms of horror of the maternal/corporeal body as gatekeeper of the natural world: "woman's womb is viewed as horrifying . . . because of its essential functions—it houses an alien life form, it causes alterations in the body, it leads to the act of birth" (49). More pressingly, though, given the film's subtext of marital breakdown, Nola's nauseating physicality connotes not only a deathly female "naturalness" but also a deep fear of the maternal bonds with which patriarchy suspects it cannot contend. Following from this, the brood's savage demeanor and revolting appearance inspire the viewer's dread that Candice—the passive, cute child—will be somehow "transformed" into one of the creatures. This suggestion is implicit in a shot of her abduction by the creatures: clothed identically and holding hands, they form a horrifyingly neat trio. Prior to Candice's abduction, Cronenberg's film momentarily withholds from the viewer a clear shot of the brood's faces, exploiting the expectations created by their innocent attire for maximum fright. Furthermore, Candice's downcast face as she is led away insinuates her own challenge to our expectations: her potential metamorphosis into one of the abominable offspring. Insofar as the film metaphorizes the battle for parental possession of children, the brood stand as metaphors for the hostile, zombielike automaton Frank fears his wife may manufacture against him (and may be herself). At the film's conclusion, Frank drives Candice away into some safe future, yet as the film closes, we see her arm dotted with watery growths. She has been irreparably traumatized by Nola, but more than this, no matter how far Frank drives her, her physical connection to her mother cannot be subverted.

Despite *The Brood*'s emphasis on a monstrously "feminized" child, there is a danger in allowing the film's stunning vision of autonomous female reproduction to obscure its parallel demonization of the child itself. The film's fear of maternal control positions the child on a continuum with psychoplasmic boils and cancers: symptoms of her mother's physical unrest. Children are further demonized in a general sense in that all the acts of evil are perpetrated by children: Nola herself is positioned as both mother and child, because when she telepathically murders her own mother, she is acting out her childhood resentment. The film's violence is connected not only with the female temper but also with children's apparently murderous irrationality.

The bloody spectacle of Nola revealing her physical mutation and birthing one of the brood forms the film's shocking visual climax and the disclosure on which the narrative's suspense depends by finally informing us where the hideous imps originated. When she lifts her nightgown, the preceding conversational close-ups drop away in favor of the camera capturing the woman's full figure as she holds her gown upward, arms almost ritualistically akimbo. Frank stands in horrified awe of this monstrous fecundity, Nola's exaggerated ability to produce children naturally enslaved to her also evoking the power and immediacy of her connection with Candice. As she tears the fetus from its blood-logged enclosure, she begins cleaning it with her tongue, obscenely showcasing maternity's natural, prehistoric relationship to childbirth, a spectacle that thoroughly belittles and renders artificial paternity's traditional emphasis on social and familial bonds. When Frank bathed his daughter (and when he discovered her bruises) he demonstrated his ability to perform a traditionally feminine role (a role evoked by a conspicuously placed bottle of pink bubble bath). Yet in one primal gesture Nola shockingly overpowers—renders laughably empty—the connection he performs. When one of the mutant brood is found dead, the theory of the bizarre creature's origin signifies a mistrust of both reproduction and female emotional stability: a detective (Michael Magee) investigating the death speculates that "some crazy woman didn't want anyone to know she had a deformed child. She's had this kid locked up in an attic for years and never told anybody. Wouldn't be the first time." The reality is much worse: a graphically "inherent" relationship that intimidatingly disorientates male parentage.

## "All of them Witches": Maternal Alienation and *Rosemary's Baby*

Until its closing minutes, Roman Polanski's *Rosemary's Baby* does not feature a child villain. And, aside from being the literal son of Lucifer, this tot hasn't time to perform any active gesture of rebellion. Nevertheless, and as the film's title suggests, *Rosemary's Baby* stresses especially the mother's ultimately nourishing relationship to her demonic offspring, and in a manner markedly different from what we find in films such as *The Bad Seed* or *The Brood*, which construct motherhood as a completely reprehensible contributor to child villainy. In *Rosemary's Baby*, the child, carried throughout the majority of the film in its unborn and thus unseen and unknown state, is finally something wrested from his mother—stealthily appropriated and reconstructed by outsiders. Because it unfolds almost entirely from the mother's perspective, the film provides an intriguing and powerful dramatization of the interference and intrusion that affect her reproductive body and threaten to re-create mother and child as devastatingly alien to one another.

When Rosemary Woodhouse (Mia Farrow) and her self-centered actor husband, Guy (John Cassavetes), land a vacancy in an upmarket Manhattan apartment building (the renowned Dakota), they are swiftly befriended by busybody—and much senior—neighbors Minnie and Roman Castavet (Ruth Gordon and Sidney Blackmer). When Rosemary falls pregnant, the announcement of her happy news brings an amplification of the Castavets' cloying interest. Yet she becomes increasingly suspicious of her eccentric elderly neighbors after overhearing ceremonial chanting through the apartment wall. A series of macabre occurrences spook her further: a female lodger staying with the Castavets is found dead outside the apartment in an apparent suicide; Guy's acting career unexpectedly accelerates after his rival is bizarrely struck blind; Rosemary's family friend, who warns her of the apartment building's occult history, falls into a coma and dies after insisting she accept a book from him with the cryptic title *All Of Them Witches*. Taking the book's title as an accusation of the Castavets as leaders of a satanic cult intent on killing her baby, Rosemary attempts to escape her domestic confines and the rigorous observation of her husband, only to be recaptured and instructed that she is merely suffering "the pre-partum crazies." Following a labor that apparently resulted in a stillbirth, Rosemary's suspicions are confirmed when she discovers that not only did her baby live and the group abduct him, but also she has birthed the infant Antichrist.

Part of the enduring appeal of *Rosemary's Baby* is certainly its willingness to leave itself open to multiple readings. Given the film's time period—which included the continued American involvement in Vietnam—we might even equate its satanic conspiracy with the threat of communism and its corruption of even the most apparently stable strata of society (in the film's final act, Roman and Minnie are said to be vacationing in then-communist Dubrovnik). At the forefront, however, is its depiction of a mother's social isolation by an obscurely archaic, masculinist tradition from which she is emotionally disconnected. Gary

Hoppenstand observes that all of "the people involved in Rosemary's pregnancy (mainly the men) want Rosemary's child for some function" (41), while Karyn Valerius goes further, arguing that "Rosemary's exploitation by her husband and the coven . . . might be read as an indictment of the more routine ways sexist social relations expropriate women's reproductive labor" (120). The viewer's isolation to Rosemary's point of view certainly suggests that we may be experiencing a fantasy of patriarchy's conniving appropriation of maternity. Attempting to escape the cult's physician, Rosemary books an appointment with her former doctor, C. C. Hill (Charles Grodin). Hill looks with blessed sympathy on his former patient: he knows there aren't really witches, but "there are a lot of nuts out there," so he immediately arranges a hospital room for Rosemary. While Rosemary rests in his examination room, however, Hill swiftly informs Rosemary's husband and the cult's obstetrician, Dr. Abe Sapirstein (Ralph Bellamy), of her whereabouts. This unsubstantiated betrayal of Rosemary by someone not actually part of the conspiracy does indeed suggest a generalized fear of the patriarchal ownership of children. We might also note that when Rosemary imagines herself raped by Satan in a dream, it is her egotistical husband who seems to transform into the prince of darkness.

Yet Polanski's film consistently refuses to function as a complete allegory. For one thing, it seems difficult to identify a satisfying metaphorical basis for Guy's surrender of his son to advance his career. *Rosemary's Baby* is indeed, as its shock ending reveals, a film about devil worshippers. However, it gains its thoroughgoing sense of the uncanny precisely from its skillful oscillation between fantasy and normality, its ability to convincingly interlace and cross-reference supernatural and routine forms of exploitation.

Other key satanic horror films such as *The Omen* (1976) and *The Exorcist* (1973) begin with a disclosure, some revelation to rock the secular comfort of their protagonists. *Rosemary's Baby* is distinguished by its protagonist's total lack of access to such avenues of meaning. The pregnancy itself proceeds largely without suspicion from Rosemary because she is rigorously quarantined from information about her own condition. Dr. Sapirstein instructs Rosemary upon her first appointment, "Please don't read books. No pregnancy was ever exactly like the ones described in the books. And don't listen to your friends, either. No two pregnancies are ever alike." Her body becomes blanched, frail, and sticklike. The incapacitating pain she feels every day is dismissed by Sapirstein as insignificant: "It'll stop any day now." Her body is so thoroughly subordinated to her conspirators' purpose that her friends have to remind her of its most basic functions: "Rosemary, pain like that is a warning that *something isn't right.*" Having little else at her disposal, she clings to the words, repeating them verbatim to her manipulative husband. Thus, the exploitation of Rosemary's body evokes maternity as a social foundation that is nevertheless conspiratorially excluded from the society it undergirds and nourishes. Following the birth and the disclosure of the child's demonic origin, Rosemary is strongly encouraged by cult leader Roman to hold onto affection for the baby to bolster the Satanists' objective: "Why don't you help us out, Rosemary? Be a real mother to him. You don't have to join [the cult] if you don't want to—just be a mother to your baby."

The Satanists' suggestion that Rosemary continue to mother her otherwise abducted child constructs for her a social identity based on exclusion that alienates and demonizes what was once carried most intimately within (indeed as a *part of*) her. That Rosemary will accept her shocking child seems inevitable. Her position is already established because the unborn child, "little Andy or Jenny," as she constantly refers to him before the birth, has ironically been carried through the film as her closest ally against the alienating conspiracy, as her sole confidant. Polanski's film constructs the child as originary representative of a demonic and inscrutable patriarchal order and maternity's only means of access or inscription into that tradition. In stunningly metaphorized form,

Figure 4.3. "Be a mother to him": in Roman Polanski's *Rosemary's Baby* (Paramount, 1968), cult leader Roman Castavet (Sidney Blackmer) offers Rosemary (Mia Farrow) a role in the conspiracy that has thoroughly appropriated her maternal body. Digital frame enlargement.

the film's adoption of a maternal perspective reveals the conspiratorial artifice of patriarchal society. For all patriarchy's nervousness over its distance from reproduction, in this film the totality of its possession of the child creates an alien and hostile space within the mother's own body.

## Conclusion

Western culture has both presumed and demanded a problematically close relationship between mothers and their children. On the one hand, women's confinement to the family home and close connection with their children has historically been appreciated as a position of social responsibility. On the other hand, alterations to the nature of this relationship have brought with them intense social fears of the child's corruption. The representations of mother and child given by the horror film illustrate both the intimate, reflective relationship women have been urged to foster and patriarchal society's profound ambivalence about the formative power of that relationship. However, *Rosemary's Baby* innovatively imagines the child's appropriation from a maternal perspective, successfully infusing macabre fantasy with social complaint. By estranging and (literally) demonizing the self-centered public discourses of men, it constructs the mother's relationship to the child as one besieged by the clandestine forces of outside, paternalistic socialization.

# 5

# Vicious Videos, Missing Mothers

## *The Ring*

*T*HE *RING* (2002), A REMAKE OF THE Japanese hit *Ringu* (1998), introduced surely the most recognizable child villain of its decade. Disavowing the ultracomposed antagonism of *The Omen* (1976) or *Village of the Damned* (1960), *The Ring* makes a point of impressing on the viewer the gruesomeness of psychic ghost-girl Samara (Daveigh Chase), clad in a bedraggled sanatorium gown from which mottled, corpselike arms dangle before they launch outward toward her victims. A sodden pelt of ebon hair obscures her entire head, falling to her waist and forming grim curtains through which she peeks her snarling, filth-caked face at the moment of attack.

The mode of this attack is noteworthy. Samara clambers up from the depths of the cathode ray tube: even as it is palpably abject, her presence flashes and fizzes with televisual static. *The Ring* gains its title from a mysterious circular formation depicted on a cursed VHS cassette whose viewers, struck down by Samara seven days after watching, are found with their mouths frozen in a traumatized gape reminiscent of Munch's *The Scream*.

Samara's combination of ghost and zombie, with (if not the genteel looks) the psychic talents of the Dayout children of *Village of the Damned*, leaves us wondering what could have produced such a wretched creature. The answer is a curious combination of maternal mistreatment and television viewing. We discover that Samara's mother (Shannon Cochran)

Figure 5.1. Televisual ghost child Samara (Daveigh Chase) emerges to claim the viewer of a cursed VHS tape in *The Ring* (Gore Verbinski, Dreamworks, 2002). Digital frame enlargement.

drove the girl's father (Brian Cox) to imprison their hated daughter in a barn with only a small TV set for company—that is, until mom finally suffocated her with a plastic bag and slung her body down a well (the dreaded ring formation is revealed as the perimeter of light emitted by its heavy stone lid). The mothers of child villains are frequently depicted as incontrovertibly too close to their children (an anxiety exemplified by the psychobiological intimacy of *The Brood* [1979] or the genetic taint of *The Bad Seed* [1956]); however, they are also frequently and shockingly not close enough, thoughtlessly distanced from their primary and "proper" work as caregivers. Cynical single mother and maverick journalist Rachel Kotler (Naomi Watts) sets about investigating the videotape mystery. She is a woman the film ceaselessly and damningly associates with Samara's mother: Rachel also has a peculiar child, who is eventually endangered by (and, in the film's 2005 sequel, actually transformed into) Samara. In its conflation of these characters, *The Ring* expresses profound anxieties about changes to women's social and familial roles and their effect on children's care and development. *The Ring* and *The Ring Two* (2005) focus anxiously on self-determining mothers alongside televisual media. With its televisual killer, recalling techno-thrillers like *Demon Seed* (1977) or *Ghost in the Machine* (1993), *The Ring* appears to be that most trendily modern of horror films, provoking concerns over the changing nature of childhood in postmodernity in light of a bombardment of televisual imagery and increasing familial disconnection. However, its confusion of maternity and media also provides a moralistic throwback to postwar anxieties about the "proper" role of mothers and television's seemingly unmanageable intrusion into the family home.

## Murderous Work: The Career Mom and the Killer

After her niece (Amber Tamblyn) falls prey to the killer video, Rachel traces the origin of the tape by searching for the sources of several images that appear on it. The mysterious film depicts a random assembly of scenes and objects whose purpose seems primarily to provoke sensations of uncanniness (unpredictable camera shifts), abjection (a box of wriggling severed fingers, a centipede snaking its way from beneath a table), and spatial disorientation (desolate locations, falling ladders). More pragmatically, though, the sights it offers form the narrative guide according to which real-life encounters with the objects depicted on the tape signify the progress of Rachel's search. One image in particular is that of a dark-haired woman who brushes her hair before a mirror, another an isolated stone well. Eventually Rachel learns that the woman is Anna Morgan, a successful horse breeder who killed both herself and her daughter, Samara, the sodden ghost child who terrorizes the video's viewers. Behind the evil child in this film lies a shocking disavowal of maternal care, a backstory that reconstructs the mother as the story's underlying villain. Upon finding Samara's watery corpse, Rachel sees (via some kind of telepathic flashback) the girl standing before a stone well singing to herself, the pastoral setting completed by the frolicking horses in the distance on which Samara's gaze is serenely fixed. Into the shot intrudes the black-clad mother, her face obscured as we hear her footsteps crunching toward her daughter: "I know things will get better," she tells the girl seconds before thrusting a plastic bag over her head. Just prior to pushing her daughter down the well, the mother narcissistically pronounces: "All I ever wanted was you."

From the film's perspective, the damning portrait of Samara's mother is prefigured by Rachel's copious demonstration of a more insidious form of maternal neglect through her status as a career woman. At the wake of her niece, who died after viewing the videotape, Rachel chats ingratiatingly with the girl's friends about smoking pot, in this way eschewing her parental authority in pursuit of the big story promised by rumors of a killer videotape. As she walks the school corridors en route to collect her son, she bellows into her cell phone at an editor colleague, "Listen, Harvey, you punctilious prick, you touch my column and I'm coming down there and poking your eye out with that little red pencil you like so much!"—finishing this abrasive display only after breaching the child-friendly confines of the classroom where her son, Aidan (David Dorfman), patiently waits. When Aidan's teacher attempts to consult her about the boy's gloomy autonomy, Rachel, having obnoxiously perched herself on a desk edge above the other woman, meets her concern with the same snappy derision she has just doled out to her colleague. Yet the film is not content to leave the connection between the two mothers at the level of suggestion. Rachel inadvertently kills a horse on her way to Samara's former home, the animal's death recalling the horses that console Samara prior to her asphyxiation. Additionally, the journalist's extreme attention to the videotape image of Samara's mother brushing her hair in a mirror implies a "reflective" relationship between Rachel and her homicidal counterpart.

The link between the mother who is not home enough and the infanticidal Anna Morgan is secured and elaborated through careful over-lapping of their children's characterizations. Rachel discovers that Samara, like her own child, was vaguely psychic. She also learns that Samara was able to inscribe photographic film mentally. As well as indicating the origin of the videotape around which the narrative centers, Samara's inscriptions recall the charcoal pictures drawn by Aidan as he waits for Rachel after class, his morbid drawings also a product of parental withdrawal. When Rachel pays a visit to Samara's physician, Dr. Grasnik (Jane Alexander), she hears Samara's psychic powers reconfigured as a metaphor for a division between parent and child that, like a disability, could be resolved through the parental patience and understanding Rachel pointedly lacks. Upon arrival at the doctor's, Rachel mistakes Darby (Billy Lloyd), a mentally disabled boy, for a waiting patient, before Dr. Grasnik explains to her that he is a permanent fixture, the child of her son. The suggestion that he lives permanently with his grandmother confronts Rachel with yet another child abandoned by his or her parents in favor of more "selfish" pursuits. The connection is clinched when Rachel asks if there was actually anything "wrong" with Samara. The doctor gestures to Darby, swinging idly on a nearby piece of playground equipment: "When Darby there was born, we knew something wasn't right with him. But we loved him anyway. It takes work, you know. Some people have limits." Rachel's guilty downward glance punctuates the point. Samara was not worse than an intellectually disabled child—indeed, no worse than her own child. The "work" required comes as a penetrating reference to Rachel's prioritization of her journalistic career over motherhood. Thus, in exploring the origins of the "evil" Samara, Rachel hears tales that echo her relationship with her own peculiar—

although certainly not evil—child, stories that shift blame away from the child and onto mothers unwilling to care "properly" for their children.

The visual depiction of the tormented Samara also appeals to Rachel's sense of guilt over her own unwanted or mismanaged child. As Rachel examines the tapes of the institutionalized Samara, the Gothic sanatorium setting connotes heartless social exclusion more than inherent illness or evil. In *Ringu*, "Sadako" (Rie Inō) is the offspring of a human and a sea creature, a supernatural lineage that goes at least some way toward nullifying the moralistic overtones of her vengeance. In *The Ring*, however, Samara has no predetermined supernatural origin to speak of— her freakishness is rephrased as a product of social neglect.

The conclusion to Rachel's journey returns her to the maternal role from which she has apparently been absent and urgently resentimentalizes the mother-child bond. Attempting to sate the avenging spirit, Rachel performs a symbolic rite of contrition with Samara's body, intimately clutching her bones in the watery grave and atoning for the sins of the abominable mother she has been investigating (and now, perhaps, sees that she is herself). So it is that the heroine of *The Ring* is not so much a heroine as a surrogate villain, and the journey she undertakes is essentially punitive: the outgoing, female investigator forced to look guiltily inward. Ruth Goldberg has pointed out that the mother in the Japanese original is driven to reassume a traditional maternal role so that family upheaval can be corrected (376). Gore Verbinski's westernized remake amplifies this ambivalence considerably, reinforcing maternal inadequacy. *The Ring*'s moralistic narrative structure is ostensibly directed toward returning the career woman to a traditional maternal role, yet its shocking denouement (the marauding Samara is not appeased by belated maternal gestures after all) snaps with the suggestion that a working mother like Rachel simply *cannot* redeem herself—she is afflicted by some inherent and irreparable maternal fault.

*The Ring Two* restates the working mother's fundamental incapacity in one of its earliest scenes, depicting Rachel's strained redomestication as a homemaker as she struggles to bake a pie exactly as prescribed in a magazine. Despite Rachel's hyperdomesticity, we still see evidence of her career's expansion beyond the family home when she annoys a male colleague by rewriting his newspaper article. Implicitly deriding her dedication, the colleague questions Rachel's ability to be satisfied with this small-time gig. Her response—"Well I'm around for my son more; in Seattle I wasn't"—explicitly evokes the unresolved tension between her ambition and her maternal role. Rachel cannot convince her son of her inherent domesticity with lousy cooking, nor can she escape the vengeful child. Early on, she hallucinates Samara lunging at her with a triumphant whisper: "I found you!" This sequel's disorganized narrative compounds our sense of Rachel's irredeemability. In this film, Aidan again accidentally watches the videotape, although not because of Rachel's careerist neglect, but because she was away from home vigilantly destroying a copy of the same tape. When her son wakes from a nightmare, Rachel rushes to console him, yet in describing his dream he cuttingly evokes her absence: "I woke up and you weren't here. You weren't here. . . ." Despite Rachel's vigilant hominess, as long as she still so much as *desires* employment outside, her home is unsettled—sufficiently destabilized for Samara to reappear.

In both *Ring* and *Ringu*, a father is also victimized, although without the corrective implications that accompany the mother's torment. In Verbinski's remake, as Aidan's estranged father scrambles around the single-guy junk of his apartment, trying desperately to evade Samara, he is a foolish but essentially blameless manchild. In fact, his death only further incriminates Rachel given that it is her failure to adequately appease the ghost child that leads to his shock victimization when all seemed, finally, safe and sound.

## Home Alone and Hating It: The Postmodern Child

Early in *The Ring*, we see a remarkably gloomy exterior shot of the high-rise edifice that Rachel and Aidan occupy produced with almost no depth of field at all, its color digitally altered for maximum blandness. The image is an eyesore and deeply expressionistic: the matching of oppressively gray sky to gray façade gives us no visual escape; it is merely a wall of anomalous industrial banality. High-rise life here is a dreadful gray purgatory, cold and inhuman. Yet a cut from this oppressively static image to a lively one of Rachel hopping around in her black underwear (and again cursing within earshot of her child) informs us of her indifference to her numbing environment and thus her implicit responsibility for it. The film singles out the kind of child raised in this environment for special interest. David Dorfman's performance as Rachel's son, Aidan, demonstrates in lugubrious caricature the results of an insufficiently "domestic" environment and routine on a child. The boy's physical pallor alone is striking; he is blanched as if vitamin deficient from his confinement to the concrete high-rise the "couple" calls home. Exponentially more morose than his Japanese counterpart, the character is transformed from an essentially normal child capable of frolicking in a stream with his grandfather to an emotionally stunted oddity possessed of a cheerless adult reserve. Aidan refers to his mother exclusively by her first name, his every syllable offered in a sulky monotone: this is the child-as-depressive. Our introduction to him, as Rachel collects him from school, stresses his apparently unnatural self-sufficiency. Concerned for this glum and overserious student, the teacher (Sandra Thigpen) informs Rachel that she "never has to tell Aidan to do anything" (meanwhile, in the background we glimpse a cutely chalk-scrawled itinerary that divides up the children's activities by day, reminding us of the dependence of normal "healthy" children on adult control). Rachel's response is incongruously snappy: "If that's a problem you'd be the first teacher in history to say so," she huffs, indifferent to the miserable autonomy of her son and dismissive of any attempt to reassert adult control—a control that, the film seems to assure us, would result in a happier, "normal" child.

As she prepares for the funeral of her niece, Rachel hollers through the house after a missing black dress. Aidan, dressed in a suit, stands elevated to nearly adult height before the mirror, not only expertly tying his own necktie, but also agonizing over its exact width and position. As he finishes, his blank gaze lingers on the mirror, the sound of the rain outside amplifying our impression that as he prepares for a funeral his independence is also something to be drearily mourned.

For Lindsey Scott, the inability of the mother to maintain her parental authority is suggested through role reversal: "Aidan in *The Ring* often assumes the role of the parent while Rachel is portrayed as the

Figure 5.2. Too much, too soon: as he prepares for a funeral, Aidan (David Dorfman) of *The Ring* (Gore Verbinski, Dreamworks, 2002) seems also to mourn his adultlike independence. Digital frame enlargement.

child. At her modern apartment home, she wears bed-shorts and a bal-
lerina tank-top as she throws her clothes around her bedroom like a
typical teenager" (16). Through this role reversal, not only does the film
recast the working mother as egotistically immature in her pursuit of
aspirations beyond the domestic sphere, but it also spitefully overlooks
economic circumstances that in fact frequently necessitate that women
seek employment beyond that sphere.

In Aidan we see an exaggerated impression of the new, autonomous child produced by working parents in the late twentieth century.
Joe Kincheloe uses the term "postmodern childhood" (170) to describe
the social changes in child rearing brought about by a steady increase
in divorce rates and an economy that gives parents little choice but to
be absent from the family home for work. "As parents are still at work
in the afternoon when children get home from school," he points out,
"children are given latchkeys and expected to take care of themselves.
Thus, we have seen generations of 'home aloners'—kids that in large part
have had to raise themselves" (159). Increasingly, children find themselves
subject to "adult" duties and responsibilities, a cultural climate that has
produced the independent child of films like *Home Alone* (1990). "In
the postmodern childhood," Kincheloe writes, "being home alone is an
everyday reality" (171), a normality also illustrated by a couple of bored
teenagers in *The Ring*'s opening scene, who in the absence of adults
bemoan in flat and ironically adult tones the harmful effects of the TV
with which they have been left alone. In Rachel and Aidan, Verbinski's
film not only depicts the child left alone (most distressingly, with the
cursed videotape) but also recasts him as part of an awkwardly modern
kind of "couple" with his mother. Unlike *Home Alone*, *The Ring*'s vision
of postmodern childhood is utterly bereft of the pleasures of autonomy.
Aidan is a gloomy, introverted insomniac, perpetually under threat from
the televisual child monstrosity.

## Anxiety Reruns from the Golden Age

What is perhaps more interesting than *The Ring* and *The Ring Two*'s
generically misogynist association of child villainy with maternal neglect
is their intermingling of those anxieties with fears surrounding televisual
media. Samara is of course quite literally the product *of* television, claw-
ing her way out of the screen and into real life. Her mode of propagating terror is decidedly self-referential: the notion of a teen-topping
videotape immediately connotes anxieties over children's access to horror
films. In particular, it reminds us of the video nasty scare of the 1980s,
when tabloid headlines foamed with outrage over the defilement of chil-

dren's minds and their hypothetical transformation into killers and rapists through easy access to a horde of cheaply produced exploitation tapes. The manner in which *The Ring* presents the tape's victims—wide-eyed, mouths hideously agape—also implies the kind of profound psychic trauma supposedly inflicted by horror media. In fact, these stretch-mouthed teen faces, in their evocation of *The Scream* (beyond signaling the film's preoccupation with the anxieties of modern life) reference Wes Craven's semiparodic *Scream* series (1996–2011), in which Munch-masked killers intend to blame their crimes on a diet of horror videos. (*Scream 3* [2000] was the big break of *Ring* screenwriter Ehren Kruger.) From *The Ring*'s opening scene, in which Samara's vengeance is first enacted on a teenager who has seen the tape, we are offered a subtle indicator of television's pervasiveness as a babysitter and substitute for parent-child interaction. Here it is the teenagers themselves who complain about the damaging effects of too much TV, while their discussion of the "illicit" videotape clearly symbolizes their access to more dubious fare. Having recently spent the weekend on a mountain vacation with a boy, one of these teens, Katie, fobs off her friend's curious inquiries by claiming that the two of them "only watched TV." This conversational strategy uses the activity as a cover for sex as well as indicating again its supervisory inadequacy; behind the convenient alibi of watching TV, the couple got up to a lot more. Katie's mother loiters ineffectively at the perimeter of this scene, her absence explicitly foregrounded by a phone call that marks the family home, the teenagers' behavior, and their eventual fate as properly within her domain of responsibility.

Television is perhaps most powerfully positioned as a deplorable replacement for familial—specifically maternal—contact in two key scenes. In the first, as Rachel recovers from the shock of seeing the cursed tape herself, she ruminates on her family's living environment, walking pensively out to the balcony and gazing around as if in contemplation of her surroundings for the first time. Alerted by the sound of booming laughter, she fixes her gaze on an apartment in which a mother places a bowl of food in front of her TV-watching child before leaving the room. Standing outside on her balcony, the woman weirdly faces the door behind which her son sits but curiously refrains from entering before casting a glance toward Rachel in a gesture of mutual guilt. This scene, strongly reminiscent of Hitchcock's *Rear Window* (1954), overlays the voyeurism of imagined communal relationships with televisual ones, depicting family interaction entirely subsumed by television. The woman's isolation of and indifference to her child foreshadows Samara's mother's confinement of her daughter and use of television as a substitute for maternal care. The second scene to clearly villainize television as a substitute for maternal care comes when Rachel and her ex-partner Noah (Martin Henderson) discover the barn to which Samara was banished: "They kept her here alone," Rachel remarks in disbelief. "Not alone," says Noah, gesturing to a battered television set. This moment serves the purpose of explaining Samara's televisual nature while pointedly associating maternal failure with the medium. Noah's grim quip implicitly references the career woman alongside him, who also leaves her son with only TV for company.

For Kincheloe, the ubiquity of TV in postmodern childhoods, a phenomenon brought about by women's increased participation in the workforce, means that children

> have gained an adult-like (not necessarily an informed) view of the world in only a few years of TV watching. . . . [As] a consciousness dominating, full disclosure medium TV provides everyone—sixty-year-old adults to eight-year-old children with the same data. As postmodern children gain unrestricted knowledge about things once kept secret from non-adults, the mystique of adults as revered keepers of secrets about the world begins to disintegrate. (171-72)

In this sense, Samara explosively emblematizes television's construction of a child with the ability (at least in Kincheloe's rather anxious description) to overturn the adult-child power hierarchy, while tying the problem back to maternal inadequacy. The proliferation of Samara's attacks—her ability to reach multiple audiences (including Rachel's son)—paranoia-cally metaphorizes television's uncontainable influence. In Samara we see a fantasy of the child's capacity to be entirely and hellishly reconstituted by the virulence of television.

In his discussion of *The Ring*'s Japanese forebear, Eric White suggests that the film ultimately positions televisual media as a radical replacement for traditional psychoanalytic narratives of identity formation:

> In the first film, the oscillating reflection of Sadako and her mother in the mirror alludes to the foundational role traditionally played by the internalisation of familial images in the formation of individual identity. But the *Ringu* films depict a social milieu in which the family matrix no longer provides the exclusive basis for psychological structure. Instead, omnipresent information technology functions as a vast psychic apparatus, or better, a psychotronic apparatus randomly propagating affec-

tive dispositions, libidinal intensities, decontextualised personae and partial selves across the social sphere. (45)

These anxieties are most trenchantly played out by the child given that it is the regulation of the child's identity that is routinely constructed as being of the highest social importance and consequence. In *The Ring*, the structure of that identity is seen as so fragile (and its stakes so high) that television's replacement of the mother can only irreparably rupture and fragment it at its core. Rather than produce a different kind of subject, the televisual child is hauntingly decentered, an unfixable specter, infectious. The damage to the child's "proper" identity is conceived as so blasphemously thorough that it infects everyone with whom the child comes into contact.

Rather than articulate a peculiarly postmodern anxiety, however, *The Ring* reactivates conservative discourses about media and motherhood characteristic of the postwar period. In 2002 the VHS technology at the center of *The Ring* was on the cusp of obsolescence, and the film's ideological disquiet similarly finds its roots in an apparently bygone era. After World War II, and concurrent with the rise of television in the home, focus on the corruptibility of childhood hit a zenith with concerns over juvenile delinquency. The figure of the juvenile delinquent gave force and tangibility to fears over the rise of mass media and its permeation of the family home. While television's potential as a unifier of the domestic sphere was praised and prescribed, its ability to pacify then contaminate the minds of youth was anxiously lamented. Juvenile delinquency was positioned as evidence that postwar women were not longer fulfilling their desired role. As Lynn Spigel points out, "[e]xperts argued that the rise in juvenile crimes during the war was largely caused by working mothers who did not properly devote their energies to their young" (115). The rise of television increasingly deregulated knowledge, threatening to disassemble the epistemological hierarchy between the child and the adult. Spigel writes, "With the mass, commercial dissemination of ideas, the parent is, so to speak, left out of the mediation loop, and the child becomes the direct addressee of the message" (114). In Samara of *The Ring* we see a child who, neglected, malnourished, and hidden in a barn in which television constitutes her only contact with the outside world, is subject to concentrated doses of the medium's supposedly deleterious effects.

The media-saturated child literalized by Samara is clearly signaled with more sobriety in Aidan: bags under his eyes give the impression of a person somehow physically altered by too much television. Advice and home-care literature in the 1950s described similar children. Spigel indicates a cartoon in *Ladies' Home Journal* that "showed a little girl slumped on an ottoman and suffering from a new disease called 'telebugeye,'" the caption describing the child as a "'pale, weak, stupid looking creature' who grew 'bugeyed' from sitting and watching television for too long" (116). The film's gloomy lighting causes Aidan's iris and pupil to comingle into uncannily large and transfixed wells of black. In *The Ring Two*, in addition to his formal shirt ensembles, he wears his hair in an anachronistic side part reminiscent of a 1950s child. In this child we can see a conservative fantasy of television's effects, while in Samara this is pushed to its cautionary, most fantastical terminus: a child subsumed by—then threateningly dispersed through—television's "contagious" influence.

## Conclusion

Despite *The Ring*'s Japanese origin, the opening of Verbinski's film leans heavily on conventional motifs of the Western horror film. In line with slasher tradition, the girls here are eroticized prior to being victimized: a fixed, low-angle close-up of their descent on the stairs ensures we get a good eyeful of bare leg. In fact, *The Ring*'s opening mise-en-scène is so clichéd (the rainy night, the teenagers, the empty house, the ringing phone) that we are encouraged to expect it will be as much a film *about* horror films as it will be one. However, the film's apparently postmodern play in the opening scene contrasts strikingly with the greater narrative's totalizing seriousness: tongue and cheek are never further apart than they are in Verbinski's film, something indicated by its unrelentingly stark lighting, willfully cryptic imagery, moody character interactions, and general humorlessness. The film's DVD release was accompanied by a documentary-style short film (*Rings*) that supplements the main narrative and in which everyone plays it dead straight. *The Ring* means business; it is a film whose horror is bereft of irony. Following from this, the stress it places on the destructive influence of televisual media and its suspicions of postmodern motherhood mark it with the unmistakable tone of censoriousness rather than send-up.

The postwar anxiety over juvenile delinquency was a crucial battleground in the contestation of changing gender roles. As Spigel writes, "the child emerged as a terrain on which to assert adult power, and the parent in turn relied on the experts' wisdom. Failure to follow this advice could result in 'problem' children or, worse still, criminals" (115). Delinquency discourse was about not only policing the child but also shunning and restricting any expansion of women's role beyond an idealized domesticity. Despite the historical context to which these concerns are seemingly tied, as women continue to pursue ambitions beyond those prescribed for them by a still predominantly patriarchal society, that society is still susceptible to paranoia over what those ambitions might lead to. John Lewis has astutely identified in *The Ring*, as well as in *The Sixth Sense* (1999) and *The Others* (2001), the reflection of a cultural shift back to conservative family values accompanying the George W. Bush administration in the United States, pointing out that conflict is created in Verbinski's film because of the incompatibility of Rachel's public role with her place in the home: "By bringing the public sphere (her work) home with her . . . Rachel inadvertently jeopardizes the lives of her son and the father of her son by allowing them to have access to the tape." Of course, the scenario Verbinski's film so scathingly describes obscures the modern workforce pressures that actually surround women like Rachel and impel their "neglect" of their children, nor does it genuinely consider their aspirational desires. It constructs children's isolation as a personal fault, seeking to reestablish mothers as what Luce Irigaray calls "the silent substratum of the social order" (47). Most potent in the film's replay of conservative hits, however, is its paranoia over television's power in the family home. The child raised within the emotional mortuary of the high-rise home is freakishly accelerated into adulthood and prey for a demonic, mediatized transubstantiation: not merely (and familiarly) vulnerable to media effects, but transformed *into* them.

# 6

# Little Bastards

## Patriarchy's Errant Offspring in *It's Alive* and *The Omen*

WHILE FILMS LIKE *THE BROOD* (1979) and *The Ring* (2002) bitterly dramatize children's corruption or contamination by their mothers, Western culture's fear of female closeness to the child not only takes the form of paranoiac fantasies; it is also answered by competing narratives of parenthood. Patriarchy has a long history of privileging the male role in reproduction in order to repair the perceived distance between father and child so traumatically evoked in several child villain films. Because the experience of biological paternity is a discontinuous one, it has increased recourse to narratives of origin that institutionalize intimacy, strengthening the perceived relationship between father and child. Traditional conceptualizations of paternity seek to override maternal closeness, interposing powerful counterimaginings that reinscribe men as the primary authors of their offspring. Consequently, several films featuring child villains are founded on crises stemming from the very constructions paternity erects against fears of its reproductive redundancy. The first part of this chapter explores how the evil child of *The Omen* (1976) overturns a patriarchal hegemony that children are ordinarily instrumental in sustaining—the child's villainy expressed through its disturbance of patriarchy's deep investment in symbolism and public roles. Narratives that draw tight the connection between father and child are nowhere more powerful than in Larry Cohen's film *It's Alive* (1974), in which the birth of a mutant child provides an unwanted reflection of its father's masculinity. The second part of this chapter examines this film's focus on masculinist accounts of reproduction, arguing that *It's Alive* plays horrifyingly on the latent signifying role of male reproductive health.

## The End Times for Patriarchy: *The Omen*

A number of prominent horror films have dusted off the grimmer implications of Christian thought to play with the idea that children might be as much a curse as a blessing. Sabine Büssing suggests that the 1968 release of *Rosemary's Baby* was followed by

> a series of motion pictures which might be aptly categorized under the term "Catholic film." The numerous examples released in the course of the last decade . . . either deal with Catholic ceremonies and doctrines or have Catholic churches as main settings. (149)

The satanic or possessed child was a brief favorite of novelists and filmmakers in the 1970s. Examples from the era include John Coyne's novel *The Piercing* and Frank De Felitta's *Audrey Rose* (the latter was the basis of the 1977 film of the same name). The popularity of the religious horror film owed in large part to the success of William Friedkin's *The Exorcist* (1973) and William Peter Blatty's 1971 source novel, far and away the best-known examples in this vein. *The Exorcist* led the way for *The Omen* (1976), which shared its predecessor's dignified approach to horror, while *The Omen* itself immediately enticed an imitator, *Holocaust 2000* (1977) starring Kirk Douglas, as well as four increasingly low-key *Omen* sequels. The success of the 1960s–70s religious horror cycle has continued to inspire somewhat nostalgic straight-to-video productions like *666: The Child* (2006) and *Whisper* (2007).

In Richard Donner's *The Omen*, ambassador-to-be Robert Thorn (Gregory Peck) is hurried to a Catholic hospital in Rome after hearing that his child has been delivered stillborn. Upon his arrival and at the suggestion of the creepy hospital *principale* (Martin Benson), Thorn consents to an exchange of the deceased for another child, conveniently orphaned that same night. It is, however, the sixth hour of the sixth day of the sixth month, and Thorn (in the wrong place at the wrong time with formidable precision) adopts Damien, the infant Antichrist: the son of Satan anticipated by the Book of Revelation (or anticipated, at least, by *The Omen's* interpretation of it). After Damien is found at the center of a series of macabre "accidents," Thorn travels to the early Christian ruins of Italy to be told that he must murder his son to prevent him from usurping his governmental prestige to bring about the Apocalypse.

One of cinema's most iconic child villains, Damien (Harvey Stephens), a sullen, black-haired, suit-wearing mute, is a remarkably subdued presence. In fact, in the loose trio of *The Omen*, *The Exorcist*, and *Rosemary's Baby*, the child is curiously neutral in the conflict in which he or she is embroiled. Damien does not instigate crisis in *The Omen*, serving merely to qualify it; catastrophes occur around rather than because of him. For the literal child of the Devil, his menace is curiously expressed through either a mere moodiness of filmic tone (emphatic close-ups, Latinate choirs) or near-coincidental mishaps that occur around him. There is little of his villainy that is not overtly reliant on a third party. His most serious misdemeanor, hospitalizing his mother, Katherine (Lee Remick), and causing her miscarriage by coasting his tricycle into the railing on which she is somewhat foolishly perched, is attributed to the nanny, Mrs. Baylock (Billie Whitelaw).[1] In the aftermath, the shot rests finally on Damien's escape from the scene, but it is a distinctly "child-like" getaway, barely coordinated. The demonization of Baylock is not nearly as ambivalent, however. Her monstrous glare fills the frame as she deliberately opens the door that will direct Damien toward his teetering mother. The really dirty business is not done by the child at all: Baylock later murders Katherine Thorn as she recovers in the hospital, dropping her from a window (her villainy again consolidated through the same intense close-up). Damien's villainy seems at its most inert after Thorn is informed that the true Antichrist will bear the mark of the beast somewhere on his body. The father steals quietly into his son's room, carefully clipping his hair to reveal a trio of sixes on the scalp beneath, while Damien remains asleep. By comparison, *Rosemary's Baby* takes this passivity to its extreme: while the same terrible offspring is essential to the narrative, a physical child is dispensed with for the majority of the film, in its place the expected, preconceived baby, the comforting idea of "little Andy or Jenny," as Rosemary refers to her unborn. In both films, conceptualizations of the child are pushed to the fore while the agency or presence of the actual person recedes into insignificance.

In this way, Damien's characterization is almost entirely articulated by his demonic contradiction to the idealized, innocent child. He gains the status of what Joann Conrad calls the "Janus-faced, good/evil child" (185). Robin Wood reminds us that classifying the repressed bogey of horror as " 'evil incarnate' (a metaphysical, rather than social, definition)" works "automatically to suggest that there is nothing to be done about it but strive to *keep* it repressed" (134, emphasis in original). Damien's supernatural status as devil incarnate ensures that destruction is the only cure for his villainy. Moreover, it conveniently removes him from the category of child as we traditionally understand it. While his villainy draws emotional power from the way it undermines entrenched definitions of childhood, his demonic origin means that those definitions can escape serious reconsideration or analysis. This child's very badness works only to preserve and reconfirm the angelic, innocent child (absent here) with whom we are familiar. Otherwise derided for its slavish adherence to the original, the film's 2006 remake, starring Liev Schreiber as Robert Thorn, heralds Damien's birth with a series of omens based on contemporary events (including the September 11 terrorist attacks and Hurricane Katrina), situating it as part of an apocalyptic avalanche that cannot be averted and lending renewed force to his inherent evil. In both films, this good/evil child duality is maintained by Thorn's tragic discovery of the skeleton of his true son, murdered at birth for the switch to take place. Not merely another assault by Damien on Thorn's family, the revelation of the tiny skeleton invokes the innocent child (Damien's polar opposite) with harrowing sentimentality: should *this* child have been the one who lived, we can be certain that he would have been every bit as angelic as Damien is demonic.

Damien's irresolvable alterity as the evil child means *The Omen* is able to use him to express a more generalized hatred of children while avoiding reflection on that hatred's relationship to any children who are real. Damien's personal villainy is largely banal; in the original film he noisily hurtles billiard balls around the table to his mother's annoyance, while in the remake he plays noisy video games instead. Such behaviors familiarize him as a typical raucous, annoying child, although one whose eradication we have license to desire without reservation. Destroying him is in fact presented to us as a moral and religious imperative. We might observe that Damien doesn't present any kind of problem until he grows up a little bit (to about the age of five), his infant charm perhaps beginning to expire; *The Omen* and its remake demonstrate to us the harmony of the Thorns' life prior to this period through a dreamy montage of family snapshots. The subtext of parenthood's inconvenience is also suggested by the spiraling affluence on which Damien intrudes. With the patriarch recently promoted, the Thorns should be enjoying the good life much more than they are. Moore's remake expands our perception of Damien as a scapegoat for the annoyance of children more generally. In this film, Katherine Thorn (Julia Stiles) expresses her desire to spend less time with her son in a moment of feminist complaint that could challenge the patriarchal management of any number of families.

However, the film's conservatism is indicated by the fact that her yearning to fulfill goals beyond childcare is valid and understandable only because her child is secretly the Antichrist.

As Thorn's prestigious position and Katherine's complaint suggest, Damien doesn't play havoc with just any idealized world in which children are best neither seen nor heard but tampers with one pointedly structured by capitalist patriarchy. Robin Wood has observed that "[*The Omen*] is about the end of the world, but the 'world' the film envisages is very particularly defined within it: the bourgeois, capitalist, patriarchal Establishment" (128). Indeed, Thorn is a paragon of upper-crust masculine authority, with Gregory Peck providing a dignifying presence that consolidates the film's straight-faced approach to a traditionally lowbrow genre. We receive several depictions of the luxuries of Thorn's status after he accepts his new position: for example, the family coasts with traffic-proof grandeur to the ambassador's residence in a Daimler Limousine (yet when mother and child take an excursion to the zoo without the patriarch, they do so in a modest two-door Datsun). A right-turn away from the mundane bustle of junction traffic, sumptuously accompanied by a romantic string melody, signifies the family's "turning the corner" into newfound wealth and exclusivity. In case this signifier of the family's upward mobility was missed, the following shot cements the Thorns' new eminence by capturing (through an ornamental trellis that restrains our plebian gaze) the car rolling up to what appears to be the ambassador's house before a surprising pan identifies the elegant building as a mere wing of his extravagant new home.

The disruption caused by Damien comes first through the imposition of an authority that supersedes that of secular patriarchy. Despite self-consciously mimicking Abraham's sacrifice in Genesis, Thorn's dramatic attempt to slay his son at the film's conclusion is not so much a dedication of faith as long-delayed necessity; should his son not have been the Antichrist, the film gives absolutely no indication of any reason why Thorn might have invited Christianity into his life (nor, indeed, why anyone would). Its rendition of religion is distinctly Gothic, intended to instill terror through the revival of beliefs that subvert the security of secular knowledge—and where what was previously unknown always turns out to be bad news. The literary Gothic has a history of putting religious discourse to use in the promotion of terror: Catholicism and papal authority provided sufficiently estranged vehicles for fears of outdated superstition and persecution. *The Omen* abounds with Gothic motifs such as patricide, ancient prophecy, secluded monasteries, and corrupt clergy. A United States ambassador is transported from the modern civility of diplomatic office work and a family stroll by an English stream to scrambling over the grim moonlit rubble of an Etruscan cemetery. The deranged priest demands Thorn take communion in a manner clearly designed to emphasize the macabre: "Drink the blood of Christ and eat His flesh, for only if He is within you can you defeat the son of the devil! . . . Accept Christ, each day, drink His blood." After he is informed that a priest is waiting to see him, Robert Thorn's cohorts chide him affably: "Donation time! I didn't know you were such a soft touch." Thorn's exchange with Father Brennan (Patrick Troughton) commences with a series of shot/reverse shots. Thorn smugly reclines in a chair framed by two flags, backed by a view of the city below, his status triumphantly visible. However, this grubby priest will show him a thing or two. "You must accept Christ as your savior," Brennan insists, his harassment of Thorn enhanced by his maddening inability to get to the point: not only is Thorn in big trouble, but Brennan all but refuses to tell him what to do about it.

The projected narrative of Damien's rise to power, and the steps Thorn must take to prevent it, challenges the father's patriarchal potency. That is, Thorn's status will be usurped should he fail to put aside wimpy sentiment and murder his own son. Instructing him on the necessity of his child's death, Italian exorcist Bugenhagen (Leo McKern) warns the ambassador in a sonorously masculine baritone: "You must be devoid of pity." Patriarchal identities are uniquely empowered in the film (given that, according to Jennings [David Warner], the nosey photographer who aids Thorn, "The Antichrist will rise from the world of politics"), and it is this quasiregal image of secular patriarchy that is under threat. Toward the film's conclusion, Thorn is reduced to creeping like a burglar around the same status-symbol house we saw earlier, in fear of the family nanny. The home has grown cavernous, dwarfing its patriarch within labyrinthine twistings of hall and stair. Moreover, Thorn must carefully evade a demonic Rottweiler brought into the house by the nanny to protect Damien, although tendered to his parents as a regular guard dog. The patrolling beast suggests an insurrection by the forces Thorn would expect to protect him from underclass riff-raff and a symbol of his failure to subjugate his (female) employee after he explicitly requested the animal's removal.

These building emasculations serve to complement the importance of the final one: Thorn, the patriarch, is unable to imitate the crime of that biblical patriarch. In keeping with the film's Gothic religiosity, his failure to dispatch Damien in a timely manner is more a matter of nerve than faith. Having found the telltale birthmark, Thorn has now received irrefutable evidence that his son is indeed the Antichrist; he drives him to a church to commit the murder but hesitates far too long—long enough to be gunned down by his own security agents. From the gloomy opening credit sequence onward, the viewer is tipped off that Damien Thorn is bad news. In accordance with the satanic thriller as Wood describes it, *The Omen* is rigorous in ensuring that we cannot consider Damien merely misunderstood, and the climax bespeaks the film's success in always keeping the boy at arm's length. At this point Damien's death is plainly necessary to resolve narrative conflict and avert Armageddon, so Thorn's hesitation evokes in us more frustration than moral sympathy, the pause inspired in him by Damien's specious innocence ("No, Daddy, no!") giving us a Thorn feebly subject to manipulation when we want him to be morally upright and dominant as all true patriarchs should presumably be.

Against the notions of personal security or dominance that psycho-analysis tends to ascribe to patriarchal identities, the work of Jonathan Rutherford addresses the precariousness of masculine relationships in their strong reliance on symbolic or abstract narratives. At the root of this investment in sociocultural representations of power is what he calls the "legacy of ambivalent paternity" (14): an uncertainty over the precise nature or importance of men's connection to children as fathers. Ruther-ford writes that "unlike motherhood, the legacy of ambivalent paternity bequeaths fatherhood with the continual fear of its own redundancy. [As a product of this] masculinity is overly dependent for its coherence upon external public discourse" (14). Damien consistently subverts Thorn's *actual* paternity, causing the death of his first child, then the death of an unborn second when he pushes pregnant Katherine Thorn over a balcony. However, Damien's supernatural origin also ensures his removal from the patrilineal relationship his father fabricates through the secret adoption, depriving the father of his status as a father. Thus, while sabotaging Thorn's literal fatherhood, Damien will usurp and abuse his father's social standing, exploiting the constructed connection between the two.

*The Omen* is largely devoid of apocalyptic spectacle. Instead, the film's drama is staged through challenges to secular patriarchy, implying the father's ultimate inability to empirically justify the extravagant author-ity to which he lays claim. The film's religious premise performs an ideo-logical sleight of hand that confuses the upheaval of male capitalist power with that of the world more generally. Moore's remake adds to the theme by depicting a Thorn ambivalent about the legitimacy of his newfound social status. Falling into the ambassadorial job after his predecessor is unexpectedly killed, the Thorn played by Liev Schreiber secretly cannot accept the legitimacy of his patriarchal role. Consequently, in this remake Damien is also symptomatic of a male suspicion that one can never truly measure up to the immense symbolic apparatus patriarchy projects.

For Wood, *The Omen* is certainly a "reactionary" horror film in that the monster's monstrosity lies in the fact that he threatens the status quo, yet the film's success can only be explained by the tacit appeal of its Armageddon: "*The Omen* would make no sense in a society that was not prepared to enjoy and surreptitiously condone the working out of its own destruction" (128–29). The idea that Damien's transgressions allow us the pleasure of witnessing the dominant ideology's catastrophic subversion is most persuasive in the film's final moments. Having effectively finished off this father, Damien links hands with the president of the United States at Thorn's funeral before stretching an impish grin for the camera (an involuntary response by child actor Harvey Stephens, initially against the director's wishes but nevertheless retained in the final cut). For Wood, the suggestion that the president of the United States has taken the Antichrist into his home is "the supreme satisfaction (masquerading as the final horror)," while Damien is the film's "implicit hero, whose systematic destruction of the bourgeois establishment the audience follows with secret relish" (128). Yet this apparently subversive node in *The Omen*'s conservatism seems dispelled by the effort the film puts into securing the viewer's identification with its patriarchal protagonist. In the film's opening scene, Thorn is nervously spirited through the night in the backseat of a stately black sedan toward the hospital in which his wife is staying, shots alternating between the front and back seat positioning us as a fellow passenger. The camera's devotion to Thorn at this moment is complemented by our access to his thoughts—their traumatic repetition of the phone call that precipitates his hurry: "The child is dead, the child is dead." Thus, the viewer is familiarized with Thorn at the rawest, most sensitive moment of his subjectivity. Point of view in *The Omen* remains closely structured around the patriarch. William Paul points out that the film "gives the impression that the father wants the son more than the mother. The father is the central character in the birth scene (not the mother), and it is the father who effectively gives birth to the child by arranging for the secret adoption of another newborn" (326). Despite the (apparent) centrality of her body to birth, Katherine is excluded from knowledge and ownership of reproduction. In the 2006 remake, Thorn is informed to his obvious distress that the birth has damaged his wife's womb and left her sterile—knowledge from which she is again excluded. The very totality of the patriarchal world of *The Omen* ensures that the viewer recognizes in Damien an antagonism that must be urgently exterminated. Thus, the moment when Damien smiles for the camera is easily read as consistent with his challenge to his father's power. Having stamped and frowned sulkily throughout the entire picture—thoroughly discharging himself from the idealized model

of childhood his long-suffering parents have desperately sought to recognize in him—this sour creature finally frames himself as an innocent
delight: with full knowledge of his impertinence, he treats us to his most
childlike grin.

## Black Majesties

Even in the case of *The Omen*, where the child Antichrist permits and
disguises hatred of any child (or all of them), the child is a curious
choice for the emblem of apocalyptic evil. Indeed, it is a choice that
films such as *Rosemary's Baby* and *The Omen* seem to make at the risk of
confining their otherworldly narratives to domestic bathos. However, the
child's unique position as a privileged representative of the social order
also ensures his or her unique ability to threaten that order and its perpetuation. Stephani Etheridge Woodson points out that "childhood is a
locus in which all of a society's internal controls function to funnel the
child into approved channels" (33): through pedagogy and socialization,
children are raised in accordance with (and, implicitly or explicitly, to
preserve) a status quo. More than this, though, the continued cultural
perception of children's inherent "purity" and "closeness to nature" constructs them as a naturalization of a dominant (and ageist) ideology. In
his 1914 essay "On Narcissism," Freud turned the lens of psychoanalysis
on to the intensity of parental love:

> [Parents are] under a compulsion to ascribe every perfection
> to the child. . . . The child shall have a better time than
> [them]; he shall not be subject to the necessities which they
> have recognized as paramount in life. . . . He shall once more
> really be the center and core of creation—"His majesty the
> Baby," as we once fancied ourselves. The child shall fulfill
> those wishful dreams of the parents which they never carried
> out. . . . At the most touchy point in the narcissistic system,
> the immortality of the ego, which is so hard pressed by reality,
> security is achieved by taking refuge in the child. Parental love,
> which is so moving and at the bottom so childish, is nothing
> but the parents' narcissism born again. ("On Narcissism" 13)

Here Freud is describing the parents' affection for the child as the nostalgic reflection of themselves when they, too, were the little "center
of the universe." The significance of childhood is bequeathed by the
parents, the parents' parents, and so on. More interestingly, though,
Freud manages to reveal that the theme of this narcissistic relationship

is already the fairy tale that romanticizes patriarchy. "He will be a great man and a hero in his father's place," he continues, "[she] will marry a prince . . ." (13). Freud overlooks the socially determined shape of these adult affections but nevertheless attributes to the child a profound role in perpetuating dominant ideology by appearing as a seemingly magical origin of social hierarchy. Children, we know, are frequently regarded as cute or perfect for appearing as miniaturized facsimiles, natural origins of a hierarchical status quo, adorable "little ladies" and "little gentlemen," like wondrous beacons of the culture that produced them.

In *The Omen*, Damien clearly looks like just such a paragon, a perfect little English gentleman. With his formal attire, Damien's dress is coded as bourgeois (even aristocratic) to the point of affectation, suggesting his conniving solicitation of adult wonder. But his prestige is entirely alienated from the ideology it appears to support in a perverse mimicry that mocks adult reliance on the child as preeminent representative of the social order. The role of the nanny in *The Omen* appears to be to deliberately play up Damien's villainous cultural majesty: "Have no fear, little one," she deferentially announces, "I am here to protect thee." The earlier scene of Damien's birthday party—complete with inflatable castle, animals, cart rides, and a merry-go-round—copiously illustrates his infant kingship.

In this scene, the suicide of the family's previous nanny is depicted as a perverse "attraction" of the fairground variety and related to Damien's greater glory. "Damien! Look at me! Look at me, Damien!—*it's*

Figure 6.1. Damien (Harvey Stephens) of Richard Donner's *The Omen* (Twentieth Century Fox, 1976), the "child majesty" amid a spectacular display of devotion his parents have organized for his birthday. Digital frame enlargement.

*all for you!"* she calls out across the manor grounds prior to jumping from the roof with a noose around her neck. The moment obscenely parodies our devotion to the child, transforming it into a motive for self-destruction. Damien is given to us as the fairy prince of bourgeois patriarchy while ultimately he refuses to perform as a true site of origin for that ideology, his childish "naturalness" naturalizing only the overthrow of the existing order.

## "Somehow the identities get all mixed up": Fatherhood, Science, and Semen in *It's Alive*

At the start of *It's Alive* (1974), Lenore Davis (Sharon Farrell) informs her husband, Frank (John P. Ryan), that the child she is carrying is well on the way. The couple then commences the giddy routine of preparing themselves for the hospital, where, as Frank rather glibly explains to their son, Lenore will "do that trick she does rather well every eleven years." Waiting in a corridor just after the birth, Frank sees a nurse run from the delivery room and collapse from a gaping neck wound. He storms inside to find his wife screaming amid an apocalypse of spattered blood and dead nurses. In fact, everyone in the room except Lenore has been gruesomely slain and the newborn has vanished. Doctors and police quickly deduce that they are dealing with some kind of killer mutant, and a hunt begins for the Davis baby as it toddles through the sewers of Hollywood, emerging to slaughter random pedestrians.

The intention of *It's Alive* is to anxiously speculate on the effect of pollution and technological advance on the unborn child. However, given the vague and unresolved nature of this science-fiction premise as well as the film's focus on the father's response to his terrible offspring, it manages to evoke conceptualizations of reproduction beyond the merely scientific. By the conclusion, we have no real understanding of the creation of a mutant child as a scientific hypothesis. However, we have seen the father's strenuous disavowal of his lethal issue followed by his deep investment in redeeming the monstrosity and preventing its destruction. If many horror commentators, most notably Barbara Creed and her followers, have emphasized the genre's centralization of the female reproductive body, the thorough confidence of *It's Alive* in male-focused accounts of reproduction evokes the monstrousness of the male body instead.

*It's Alive* clearly positions the mutant child as a paternal responsibility. After the Davis baby escapes, a doctor and policeman question Lenore and Frank in an attempt to identify what this child might be, suspecting some bizarre "genetic damage." A low-angle shot allows the viewer a chance to adopt the silent Lenore's perspective, giving us a good view of her husband's much too indignant outburst, "Can you believe they're trying to blame us?!" We must note that it is Frank who is peculiarly attuned to any implication of blame; he aggressively answers questions that have really been directed toward his wife and refuses to undergo a physical examination. This assumption of paternal authorship draws on historical (yet still latently perpetuated) accounts of reproduction that privilege the male role, considering him the supplier of the infant's spirit or human core while the woman contributes housing or mere material. In her book *Sperm Counts: Overcome by Man's Most Precious Fluid*, Lisa Jean Moore traces the cultural conceptualization of sperm from its attributed theological origins to the claims of modern scientific discourse. Thomas Aquinas, she notes, followed Pythagoras's and Aristotle's notion that fathers contributed the "essence" of their offspring: in Aquinas's discourse, "semen's intention is to produce a replica of itself, a male. Apparently, though, if the semen is 'weak' or if environmental factors are not precipitous, a female might get created instead" (20). For Aquinas, semen was sacred. Not only did it contain an already fully formed microscopic human, but it held also "a (vital) spirit . . . a certain heat derived from the power of heavenly bodies" (qtd. in Moore 20). The idea that each spermatozoa contained a preformed human continued into the seventeenth century, when it was ineffectually rivaled by theories that the homunculus was contained in the ovum instead; thus, in this era, women were reverted to the role of "'mere vessels' in the context of human reproduction" (21).

Patriarchal notions that interpret sperm as "seed"—and thus containing all essential generative power—remain powerful in Western culture. Certainly, popular culture tends to anthropomorphize sperm as "little guys" or "little swimmers," and cartoons and reproductive learning aids humanize them relative to ova. Popular culture's anthropomorphization of sperm often idealizes it as an expression of hegemonic masculinity—as, for instance, "little soldiers" (see Moore and Durkin 82 and, as a counterpoint, Woody Allen's all too timid spermatozoa in *Everything You Always Wanted to Know about Sex* [1972]). Following this logic, a sperm-as-seed view of reproduction is clearly and horrifyingly played out in *It's Alive*. Because patriarchal discourses of origin tend to reconstitute mothers as the anonymous (and unpaid) production-line operators of the community and attribute essential generative power to men, the scenario depicted in Cohen's film forces a sudden concentration on the imagined cultural value of the male body. Whereas fatherhood is often seen as a connection sustained primarily at the level of public discourse (something evidenced in *It's Alive* through Frank's hearty communion with other men in the waiting room where he awaits the validation of his male fecundity), it has now become ambivalently corporeal. As Frank brushes his teeth, he nervously contemplates his reflection in the mirror, the tremors of the handheld camera here emphasizing his suddenly unfamiliar form. Ideologies of paternity seem to have uncannily re-created his material body into something monstrous.

From Frank's self-conscious perspective, Lenore, the vessel who "does [that trick] rather well every eleven years," is not implicated in the monstrosity, while the deformed child thrusts the father's now apparent inferiority into hideous, shameful view.

## Semen Stains

The birth of Frank's monstrosity thus constructs sperm as a physical expression of male social worth, a signifier operating within a public, hierarchical schema of masculinity. The perception of sperm as an index of one's heteronormative masculinity has been most powerfully (and degradingly) evoked in cases of male infertility. "An important part of the experience of male infertility," writes Moore, "is the projection of

Figure 6.2. Frank Davis (John P. Ryan) nervously contemplates the recoding of his physical body following the birth of his monstrous child in Larry Cohen's *It's Alive* (Warner Bros., 1974). Digital frame enlargement.

the sperm's characteristics onto the men who produce them (weak, slow, invalid)" (29). Culturally, the effort of men who do not produce optimum sperm may be described as "shooting blanks," while fertile sperm is "live ammunition" (Moore 28). The connection of sperm with the ideals of heteronormative masculinity doesn't reside only at the level of folk discussion on semen quality but can be perceived even within more modern medical discourse. Moore illustrates this through the example of Richard F. Spark's 1988 book *The Infertile Male: A Clinician's Guide to Diagnosis and Treatment*, which "includes a chapter encompassing sophisticated techniques for medically managing infertility entitled 'Coping with the Hopelessly Infertile Man.' The use of the terms 'coping' and 'hopeless' indicate the threat to masculinity that is assumed by the lack of fertility" (28). In short, the questioning of the quality of one's sperm specifically is also the questioning of one's manhood generally.

The birth of the mutant Davis baby also triggers a decisive patriarchal demotion for his father when Frank is fired from his job. With compulsive zeal, he informs the authorities hunting the child that he has another son, "perfectly healthy, brilliant in school"; that in principle he's "just like everybody else" in wanting to destroy the mutant. These assertions are attempts to resolve the issue of his genetic quality and thus find his way back to masculine inclusion. Frank's other son, with whom he shares an affectionate fatherly moment in the film's opening scene, stays with a surrogate father figure for the majority of the film lest he find out about his mutant sibling. On the phone with Frank, the friend encroaches onto Frank's paternal territory, offering to take the boy to the lake as well as mouthing a subtly cuckolding request for Frank to pass on his love to Lenore. As Frank prepares a revolver to join in the hunt for his child, his wife indicates the unconscious logic of his quest: "Why are you so anxious to be the one to do it?!" Through a triumphant display of hegemonic masculinity, Frank seeks to supersede and obscure his masculinity's spectacular public degradation.

A medical research institute's offer to Frank to sign the monstrous child away to science explicitly makes him monstrous himself. "It's not my child," Frank tells the university representative as he signs the contract. The representative encourages this negation: "That's very wise— disassociate yourself emotionally." The deal, however, is dissatisfying in its recourse to a Frankensteinian definition of fatherhood that still negatively implicates Frank. "I suppose that's going to be in all the medical journals," he mutters, "[and] history books, huh? The 'Davis Child.' The 'Davis Monster': like Frankenstein." He goes on to explain that he used to think that the title of James Whale's *Frankenstein* (1931) referred to the monster ("Karloff walking around in these big shoes, grunting"); it was only after he reached high school and read Mary Shelley's novel that he realized Frankenstein was the creature's creator: "Somehow the identities get all mixed up, don't they?" Despite the university professor's suggestion that he "not allow [himself] to be oppressed by escapist fiction," the deal mingles Frank("-enstein") into the creature's public identity, recreating him as a socially maligned specimen. The title of *It's Alive* thus evokes James Whale's adaptation of *Frankenstein* not only through the film's ambiguous mad-science thesis but also through the confusion of monstrousness between father and child.

Frank's eventual desperation to "redeem" the monstrosity he has sired and rescue it from destruction, while presented by the film as a humanistic change of heart, disguises his attempt to reconceptualize the baby in a way that will salvage his masculinity. In the film's climax, a reverse-tracking shot captures Frank sprinting through a sewer tunnel with the creature in his arms, a (male) "delivery" of the creature from the waste-filled womb of the industrial state and the authorities' intention that it be cornered and destroyed ("aborted") there. In accordance with the film's patriarchal understanding of reproduction, in which women contribute mere (construction) material to babies while men supply the plan and kernel of humanity, Frank represses the creature's monstrousness, championing its "essential" (male) normalcy.

*It's Alive* highlights the power of patriarchal "sperm-as-seed" notions of paternity and the latent value of this in legitimizing male social status. Moore writes that "declining sperm counts matter to the social body as well as to individual bodies" (26), highlighting the stigmatization of men through their disqualification from hegemonic masculinity. Similarly, the production of a mutant child has humiliating social consequences, resubstantiating one's public identity as a failure of heteronormative manhood. Through his imagined connection to the child, Frank is marked as inadequate or inferior among his peers, excluded from a hegemonic masculinity that supports itself through exaggerated notions of its own importance in reproduction.

The reflection of monstrous births back onto their fathers is continued in the sequel, *It Lives Again* (1978). As Eugene Scott (Frederic Forrest), the father of one of the monstrous children, lovingly envelops his wife (Kathleen Lloyd) from behind as they prepare for bed, she emits a series of pointed exhalations before finally squirming from his embrace. He is moved to interrogate her: "Makes you feel *sick* when I touch you now!? Makes you feel sick because of what we created?" His moist-eyed wife cowers against the wall—"No, I don't know!"—unable to conceal her desire to evade Eugene's contaminated sexuality. *Island of the Alive* (1986) conflates this semen-horror with contemporary cultural anxieties surrounding HIV infection. A prostitute (Laurene Landon) is horrified to discover that Stephen Jarvis (Michael Moriarty), one of her clients, previously fathered one of the deformed babies. Prior to her discovery, as the couple have sex surrounded by myriad plush toys from the carnival where the hooker met her Johns, Jarvis seemed transported back to an awkward adolescence: "You're like a high-school kid!" the woman jests. His wife having left him, Jarvis has already been stripped of his heteronormative status, this encounter with the prostitute clearly framed as a replaying of the loss of his virginity and acquisition of "adult" masculinity. "Since this is such a big night in your life, let's make it *very* special" she offers. He proceeds with the rite of passage. However, when the woman discovers his paternal history, she rages at the possible pollution of her body. His sexuality enduringly tainted and the object of stigmatization and disgust, Jarvis is doomed to remain stalled at the perimeter of the manhood he desires. Later in the film, on an expedition to the island where all of these killer babies are now kept, Jarvis makes openly juvenile advances on a female expedition member, advances through which he maligns his own credentials as a suitor: "You know you're very beautiful, maybe it's the environment but you turn me on. And I could turn you on. You've seen my kid haven't you? That's just a glimpse of the animal in me." The birth of his child means he can only grasp with parodic disaffection at the masculine status he desires, angrily offering his paternity only as a monstrous exaggeration of manhood.

In *It's Alive*, the male responsibility for reproduction is significantly exaggerated through the role of medical authority. Robbie Davis-Floyd and Joseph Dumit have discussed the rise in emphasis on what they call the "baby-as-product" in Western societies, a result of the increased promotion of synthetic hormones for speeding labor and technologies available for assessing fetal "quality" (5). This baby-as-product is implicit in the cultural landscape of the film, indicated by Lenore's suggestion to two medical specialists that "maybe it's all the pills I've taken over the years that've done this." In this medical-economic macrosystem, "desirable" children are increasingly perceived to be the product of medical or social intervention. For Davis-Floyd and Dumit, these developments contribute to a "technocratic" model of birth, a notion that "parallels the Cartesian doctrine of [a] mind-body separation" (6) that is emphasized by the normative separation of child from mother in a bassinet for observation after delivery: "In this way, society demonstrates conceptual ownership of its product" (6). The technocratic conceptualization of babies as "separate" or "the product of a mechanical process" implies "that men ultimately can become the producers of that product (as they already are the producers of most of Western society's technological wonders)" (6). Fatherhood's investment in institutional and cultural forms is thereby reinforced through the perceived "necessity" of medical/state interference in childbirth. The scene in which Frank stares affectionately through the glass of a partitioned room where a number of identical babies lie sleeping in plastic bassinets emblematizes this increasingly state-controlled conception of childbirth: the children shown here are clean, organized, identical, and dependent on medical intervention. Window-shopping, Frank expresses aloud his desire to "have one like that." The credence lent to medical interference to give and sustain meanings of reproduction exaggerates men's contribution to, and responsibility for, their offspring. The film gives us a conflation of ideologically aligned discourses: first, the male social control of reproduction is conflated with biological origin, then the dominance of this way of thinking is reflected onto and reconstructs accepted views of the male body.

Interpretation of the bloodthirsty baby is central to *It's Alive* (a question specifically emphasized by Frank's changing attitude to his offspring): is such a being truly to be regarded as a "monster"? However, the articulation of its monstrousness is deeply determined by its relationship to (and ability to be finally co-opted into) discourses of heteronormative masculinity. The killer baby is an admittedly sensational and gratuitous device. Yet the film's serious treatment of the emotional crisis it triggers reveals the conceptually unstable nature of reproduction in the public sphere, illustrating a latent hierarchical masculinity based on one's imagined sperm quality.

## Conclusion

The horror film's child villains frequently occur as paranoid symbols of women's closeness to their children, either through reproduction or through their status as primary carers. The child's villainy may be forged through an "inexcusable" withholding of female care. Alternatively, women may be reviled for being *too* close, for imbuing children with some malevolent germ that paternity can neither comprehend nor access. The common denominator is patriarchy's conventional insistence on managing and mediating the relationship between mother and child. In both *It's Alive* and *The Omen*, the chill comes from the shocking disruption of patriarchy's confident management of reproduction. *It's Alive's* obscure and undeveloped suggestion that Frank's sperm may have been contaminated swells through the presumed totality of male authorship, developing into a horror of the male reproductive body—a full-blown crisis of masculinity with profound personal and social implications. As Moore and Durkin write, advances in reproduction that scrutinize and evaluate sperm quality with reference to the criteria of hegemonic masculinity mean that "men are being constructed as driven and defined by their sexuality and male bodies—with their motives and essential 'nature' recognizable by their bodily fluids—as female bodies have similarly been constructed" (87). Additionally, the film depicts a milieu in which technological mediation of reproduction increasingly abets the effacement of the female role. As a number of feminist theorists have pointed out, reproductive science's tendency to appropriate reproduction for men has been recently aided by ultrasonic representational procedures that depict the fetus as an autonomous entity, recasting the mother's body as mere "background" and thereby overlooking the intimacy and irrevocability of her connection (see Petchesky, Rothman). Encased in Frank's fatherly pride (jovially demonstrated at the start of *It's Alive* as he banters in the waiting room) is his expected confirmation of his heteronormative status, his triumphant adherence to a hegemonic ideal. However, his assumed centrality in reproduction serves instead to disastrously eject him from the masculinity whose potency, through fatherhood, he expected to proudly demonstrate.

Superficially, there is nothing too convincing about *The Omen*. Dangerous dogs are used as the somewhat Draculean earthly servants of Satan; our view of Father Brennan's invisibly triggered death recalls the all-seeing cauldron of *The Mummy* (1932) more than it does any biblical evil; the term "episcopal" is used interchangeably with the term "Anglican"; the Bible belonging to Thorn's sidekick, Jennings, is splayed at the center while Jennings inexplicably reads from the concluding Book of Revelation (which, of all people, the film's priest erroneously pronounces "Book of Revelations"). The effect and endurance of Donner's film is contained not so much in its "Armageddon" as in its convincing picture of a man brought to the brink of despair—its symbolization of total social and familial crisis as a supernatural one. Damien's depiction is deeply wrapped up in the child's expected perpetuation of social norms and values. As Jens Qvortrup writes, children's

> definition in modernity is strongly characterized by our expectations as to their futurity as adults. Colloquial expressions such as 'children are the future of society,' children are the next generation' and 'children are our most precious resource' tend

to deprive them of an existence as human *beings* in favour of an image of them as human *becomings*. . . . (5)

Yet in Donner's film, the tidy little gentleman only uncannily parrots social hierarchy, inverting the child's role of perpetuating and mystically naturalizing male power.

# 7

## Past Incarnations

### *The Exorcist* and the Tyranny of Childhood

About two thirds of the way through *The Exorcist* (1973), the doubting priest and seminary psychiatrist Damien Karras[1] (Jason Miller) stares through wired glass into the cavernous room of a psychiatric hospital, searching painfully for his recently committed mother. From his perspective we see only another elderly woman, statue still, staring through a window whose wan light casts the pattern of its latticed metal screen over her face and body—over literally everything in the shot. There is another unmoving patient, her gray eyes matched to the sodden gray of the walls; still another stretches her mouth to a silent gape as she traces invisible shapes on her bedsheet; and another, bluishly pale, lies with her eyes open on a bed, inert as on a mortuary slab. Yet another woman, her eyes clamped shut, rubs her face, kneading the reddened skin around. Our attention is diverted to the uncle (Titos Vandis) standing alongside Damien (though not bothering to look in), who pipes up to casually blame the priest for his ailing sister's environment: "You know it's funny, if you wasn't a priest you'd be [a] famous psychiatrist now on Park Avenue. Your mother, she'd be living in a penthouse instead of there." As Damien ventures into the room, the patients drift toward him like hungry spirits. One pulls the clerical collar from his neck before being escorted away by a nurse, emitting an anguished wail that persists in the background as Damien reaches his mother (Vasiliki Maliaros) at the back of the room.

117

With moistened eyes he addresses the woman who bore him: "Momma . . . It's Dimi, momma." The mother, in restraints on her bed, and with eyes raw from weeping, rolls her head in her son's direction. At the moment of recognition, however, Damien is heartbreakingly rebuked. "Dimi . . . Why you do this to me, Dimi? Why?" Damien moves swiftly to her side, attempting to gently turn her averted head toward him, to embrace her despite the obstacle of the bed rail and the restraints. "Momma, I'm going to bring you home. Everything's going to be all right." She rambles and whimpers in her native Greek as he continues his pleading. However, her resistance is total.

Outside, and perhaps hoping that his mother's condition is no more than a symptom of her environment, Damien implores the uncle, "Can't you put her someplace else?" The uncle grins condescendingly. "Like where? Private hospital? Who got the money for that, Dimi?—*you?*" No, he doesn't. And his mother soon dies.

It is difficult to recall a bleaker, more harrowing depiction of child guilt in film, of the guilt of having ignored, disappointed, or forsaken a parent, of having done nothing when a parent is in torment. Yet the scene is also suffused with Damien's latent anger at the uncle's and mother's ignorance of his desire and intention to do *everything*. Moreover, earlier we witnessed Damien's journey to his mother's house, where he ate and

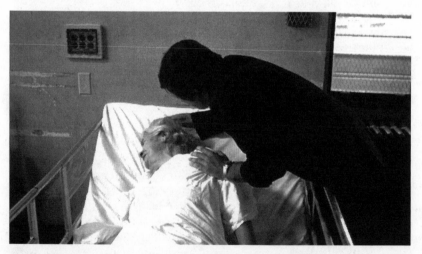

Figure 7.1. Father Damien Karras (Jason Miller) pleads for the affection of his ailing mother (Vasiliki Maliaros) in William Friedkin's *The Exorcist* (Warner Bros., 1973).

talked with her, tenderly bandaged her injured leg, and put her to bed. In her dementia, however, she not only does not recognize but also demonizes her son, inventing for him an ingrate persona that is shockingly inaccurate if beyond easy correction because of her mental condition. So heartachingly thorough is her emotional disposal of "Dimi" that she will not even look at him, shirks his very touch (the touch hungrily sought by the other women, who have no such visitors), and refuses to speak the same language.

There is of course another character in *The Exorcist* who is subject to intrusive medical interference, who must remain strapped to her bed, and whose dramatic suffering Damien feels helpless to abate. The spectacle of the possessed twelve-year-old Regan MacNeil (Linda Blair) is by now legendary to filmgoers and pop culture fans. Her face rewritten with necrotic pallor, her cracked skin, her multiple infections, her steamily putrid exhalations rising in the frigid air of the bedroom to which she has been forcibly confined: all of these are iconic. The vocal register of a cheerful eleven-year-old has plummeted to a roiling bellow; communication has been reduced to sardonic mimicry and outbursts of derision, obscenities, and celebrated quantities of green slime. For Mark Kermode, the early scene in which Damien visits his disturbed mother serves to suggest that "the psychiatric patients' illnesses may somehow be spiritually derived, but also that Regan's 'possession' might be nothing more than yet another form of psychological disturbance" (40). However, the powerful foregrounding of Damien's relationship with his mother performs more than a mere foreshadowing of the uncertain nature of Regan's possession. This mother-child encounter looms torturously over the priest's meeting with Regan, who not only reminds him of his own "betrayal," perversely mimicking the voice of his mother ("Why you do this to me, Dimi?") but also presents herself as a notably hideous version of the "bad child."

Adapted from William Peter Blatty's best-selling novel of the same name, *The Exorcist* garnered ten Academy Award nominations, becoming one of the highest-grossing and most culturally significant horror films of all time.[2] William Friedkin's film is surely the most recognizable of all evil child films, having influenced scores of religious-themed horror pictures (*The Omen* [1976], *Manhattan Baby* [1982], *666: The Child* [2006], and so on). It has been approached from a multitude of critical perspectives. Perhaps the most significant of these have been the ones that prioritize the gender of its characters. Tanya Krzywinska suggests that "Karras's determination to save [Regan] from the clutches of the demon . . . fuels a classic male fantasy of rescuing the beleaguered child or woman" (256). More pointedly, Barbara Creed fixes attention on the possession's exaggeration of "obscene" bodily functions—on Regan's festering, drippy, over-sexed body—using the film as an example of the "monstrous-feminine" in horror (31–42). By contrast, William Paul reads the film largely in terms of childhood regression. For him, Regan's bodily chaos and indifference to sexual norms present a regression that the viewer needs to see punished. This bodily rebellion (regurgitation, masturbation, urination) is representative of generalized social anxieties surrounding children and symptomatic of the period in which the film was released (310). Kermode also comments on a broad climate of social unrest, seeing in the film "on one level, a paedophobic tract, reflecting deep-seated parental anxieties about the changing nature of 'childhood'" (27). While I have no quarrel with these interpretations, their tendency to hold the film at a remove, situating it as a generalized artifact of social unease, diverts attention away from specific and symbolically rich forms of anxiety that it dramatizes. In fact, both streams of critical thought have tended to obscure *The Exorcist*'s distinct and intriguing establishment of a connection between the male priest and the female child that is not so much adversarial—based on the horror of sexual difference or youth rebellion—as consonant. Approaches to the film that integrate the narrative as a symptom of social unease downplay the centrality of the distressing personal narrative established between Father Karras and his mother. I want to refocus attention on *The Exorcist*'s overlooked association of Regan with Damien Karras himself, arguing that Regan's possession is an explosive metaphorization of Damien's feelings of villainy in his relationship with his ailing mother, of his debilitating conception of himself as a transgressive child. The possessed child in Friedkin's film is not, as critics have implied, so much Other as it is powerfully, obscenely, the same: symbolically a facet of its tortured protagonist that he is unable to relinquish.

## Little Dimi

The trope of possession allows *The Exorcist* to present a child villain while preserving the dominant, romantic image of the child we know and love. The demon inhabits the child's body, contorting it to its perverse desires, but does not (one hopes) irrevocably contaminate it. In short, the two subjects are distinguishable, as Regan's mother clearly points out: "I'm telling you that that thing upstairs is not my daughter." The exorcism ideally banishes the offending element, leaving the precious remainder intact. At the film's conclusion, Regan importantly "doesn't remember anything." However, lest the demon's innocent ransom be entirely overshadowed for us by the barking, spew-spattered spectacle of the possessed

Regan, the film secures our investment in the precious, innocent child at several key points. As he examines audio recordings of Regan's possessed voice, for instance, Damien first hears Regan's phone call to her father in all its rambunctious cuteness. On another night, Damien is called to examine the words "Help me" scrawled on the girl's abdomen—a message from the suffering child within. Perhaps the most aggressive reinforcement of Regan's innocence and need for protection comes through the medical testing she endures prior to Damien's arrival on the scene. Her mother is situated behind a screen, a helpless spectator, a number of shot/reverse shots between the two drawing us into her parental anguish. The nostalgic conceptualization of childhood underscored here evokes Freud's "child majesty": the construct through which the adult enjoys in the child the narcissistic reflection of the time when she, too, was most celebrated by her parents. Enticed by an aura of wonder and potential, the adult disavows the demands of reality, seeking a kind of nostalgic relief and safety by, as Freud phrases it, "taking refuge in the child" ("On Narcissism" 13).

However, through the character of Damien Karras, *The Exorcist* also develops a darker side to this idealization. For Damien, notions of the innocent, nostalgic child have achieved oppressive weight and haunting power. It is his mother's view of him that looms over his meeting with Regan and the maternal gaze through which the spectacle of Regan's possession must be interpreted. We first see Damien when he is spied by Regan's pointedly secular mother, Chris (Ellen Burstyn), as he professes doubts about his faith near the church where she lives ("There's not a day in my life that I don't feel like a fraud . . ."). The moment ropes the viewer in with a surprisingly personal disclosure, demystifying the priesthood and piquing our interest in the enigmatic Damien's personal conflict. The narrative focus dislocates from Chris to Damien at this point and proceeds to intimately connect his doubts about his vocation with his self-conception as an inadequate child.

A scene on the subway tips us off fairly quickly to his attachment to an image of wondrous innocence that he is terrified of having besmirched. The subway is a cavern of crackling electricity and rumbling steel, neon and fluorescent lights illuminating the stark metallic and concrete forms as the camera traces Damien's path through the pylons. The station is almost deserted as he waits. Farther down the platform we see a couple of elderly women as the track zaps and fizzes and a silent jet of steam emanates over the track. Suddenly a voice: "Father! Will you help an old altar boy?" Slumped on the ground against a wall and semiobscured by the darkness, a haggard derelict motions with hand extended as he groans, surrounded by garbage, newspapers, runnels of his own piss extending obscenely across the dirtied concrete behind him. "I'm a Catholic." The rushing train from behind Damien illuminates the vagrant's grizzled visage. The insistent, unblinking eyes pinion the priest. Damien gazes back, his face locked in an anguished frown, before he escapes onto the train, having given the man nothing. The vagrant explicitly presents himself as a kind of "fallen child," and Damien simply cannot bear the horrific contrast between the sacred innocence to which the man appeals and his mottled, piss-soaked state.

The priest's journey through his mother's dilapidated neighborhood prefigures our knowledge of his decision to pursue a psychiatric career within the unprofitable confines of the priesthood. The street where his mother lives contrasts starkly with the ones through which the affluent Chris strolled earlier, expressionistically detailing Damien's internalized persona as the not-good-enough son. Children jump on car hoods; a crossing sign emblazoned with icons of an adult and child can be seen as he crosses the street alone before reaching the apartment. As Damien turns the key to his mother's place, a baby wails over the soundtrack, evoking his return to the domain of his childhood. In fact, his entrance is curiously drawn out. As he faces the direction of a crucifix mounted on her wall, he inspects his clerical collar; then, turning again to face the trophies and photographs, he removes it altogether, placing it on the tabletop alongside the mementos, including a prominently displayed childhood photo of Damien.

Figure 7.2. Damien Karras's (Jason Miller's) clerical collar, positioned foremost among totems of his mother's pride in William Friedkin's *The Exorcist* (Warner Bros., 1973). Digital frame enlargement.

Through this deliberate placement of the collar next to the photographs, we perceive that in his role as priest, Damien still desires to be the "good boy" of his mother's memory. She greets him zealously, gripping his cheeks like the child she still imagines him to be: "Dimi, Dimi!" Yet he leaves her company frustrated by her refusal to relocate despite her worsening condition. Despite having placed his collar on the mantle as a token of "Dimi" the good boy, Damien afterward reframes his occupation as a tacit contributor to his mother's deterioration when at the bar with his buddy, Tom (Thomas Bermingham): "It's my mother, Tom, I never should have left her." In the wake of her devastating renunciation of him, Damien's faith absents him more forcefully, becoming a cruel burden in his quest to forever be the child of his mother's wishes.

## "Why you do this to me?"

Damien's anxieties come home with shocking force in the spectacle of the possessed Regan. Upon first meeting him, Regan first mimics the voice of the sickly vagrant, again confronting him with that degraded "child": "Can you help an old altar boy?" Later she faultlessly mimics the voice of his mother, repeating the traumatic accusation: "Why you do this to me, Dimi?" Beyond reminding Damien of his guilt, the question now horrifyingly doubles as a reference to the decrepit, repulsive figure of Regan herself, as if Damien's mother asks with Regan's mouth: *Why have you become for me this horrible child?* The doctor's explanation to Chris that so-called "possession" "begins with a conflict or a guilt" applies noticeably more to Damien than to Regan herself (who has nothing that we know of to feel guilty about); Regan's offensive appearance and behavior symbolize Damien's feeling of monstrousness in the eyes of his mother—symbolize what he has done to "Dimi," the good boy. During a scene in which a psychiatrist attempts to therapeutically hypnotize Regan, requesting that the demon within her "come forward" and answer him, a photograph of Regan as a younger child is mysteriously knocked from the mantle. This is not only another in a long line of affronts to the darling child Regan used to be but also a reference to the proud photographs of the young Damien from earlier in the film—an equation of the demon with the destruction of the idealized child of the parents' memory. In this sense, critical treatments of the film have overlooked the connection between "being possessed" (by negative forces) and what we speak of as "possessive" love, such as that of Damien's mother for her son. In the film's prologue, we saw the aging archaeologist priest, Father Merrin (Max von Sydow), who will eventually attend to Regan, come face to face with a statue of the possessing demon Pazuzu in the desert of northern Iraq. Now, as Damien enters his mother's house and puts down his collar, a *National Geographic* magazine sits curiously alongside the trophies and photographs, reminding us of the film's exotic opening location and linking Damien's glorified childhood with diabolical menace. Similarly, the elevated gold trophy in this shot evokes the elevated Pazazu monument, the moment at which demonic forces are first symbolized; the relics responsible for demonic possession in Friedkin's film are ultimately the relics of childhood.

The tellingly named minor character Lieutenant Kinderman (Lee J. Cobb), who appears on the scene to investigate a possible murder and some church vandalism, proves to be one of the film's most pointed ways of associating the "bad" child Regan with the priest. His official concern is the murder of a man named Burke, a romantic interest of Regan's mother who was hurled from Regan's window in a crime that is never definitively resolved. Kinderman's supposition that the crime was committed by a "very powerful man" immediately recalls Damien, an amateur boxer. Damien certainly did not creep into Regan's room and murder a stranger, yet his guilt is suggestively evoked. The lieutenant suspects that the vandalism of a statue of the Virgin Mary in the church and the murder were both committed by "somebody with a spite against the church, [and part of] some unconscious rebellion." Damien, who certainly fits the bill, catches his drift: "A sick priest, is that it?" While Damien claims not to know anyone who fits the lieutenant's description, we can scarcely repress the pertinence of the lieutenant's comments to Damien's own anxiety over his occupation and to the priest's relationship with the mother from whose affections he was so resolutely excluded. The Virgin is also linked iconographically with the old mother: earlier, as Damien entered her living room, we glimpsed a prayer table bearing a statue of the Virgin Mary along with another dimly lit picture depicting the Madonna on the back wall. Thus, we can note that the vandalism takes the form of an attack on the idealization of the mother, an outburst that matches the emotional violence Damien believes he has perpetrated.

*The Exorcist*'s unusual narrative rhythm is also instrumental in forging a symbolic connection between Regan and "Dimi." Paul has observed that

> One broad strategy [of the film] necessitates a certain amount of construction on the part of the audience: the establishment of a narrative line that seems to be cut off before it is fully worked out. As a result, each individual segment of narrative operates much like a suspension in music, by hovering

over the next segment that is introduced, thus setting up an expectation of resolution in the audience. (298)

The juxtaposition of several scenes involving Damien anticipates Regan's possession as being demonic, not medical, and foreshadows the intersection of the two subplots. Crises in Damien's narrative frequently manifest in some advance in Regan's possession, legitimizing the paranoid suggestion that Damien's lapse in faith is directly responsible for what happens to the girl. As Damien confesses his loss of faith to Tom at the bar, the scene ends abruptly, the shift to a tempestuous argument in the MacNeil house unconsciously attributing family breakdown to the ebb and flow of Damien's emotions. Later, the priest, in mourning for his mother and held in a depressive pause, struggles to perform the Eucharist while, elsewhere, Regan struggles against a team of doctors; a quick cut back to Damien, eyes set in a contemplative downward glance, suggests he is looking quite precisely *at* the girl, envisioning the outcome of his failure in her agony.

These parallels constantly work to repair what is potentially the film's most pressing omission. Why, of all people, is Regan targeted for demonic occupation? The film's narrative structure intimately sutures Regan's degeneration to Damien's own anxiety, encouraging us to find some unstated connection between the two. The meticulous symbolism of Friedkin's film equates Damien's loss of faith with his failure to live up to the image enshrined by his mother, the crisis that prefigures Regan's possession and spectacular transformation into the abhorrent child. *The Exorcist*'s narratively dispersed and rhythmically clipped scenes channel emotional tension into the climactic spectacle of possession. It is not clear what unearthed artifacts or priestly doubts have to do with a preteen in Georgetown: the film ultimately coheres as a frustrated assembly, the chaotic expression of which is demonic possession.

The romance attached to the child majesty is nostalgic. This seems to be what literary scholar Reinhard Kuhn refers to when he speaks of an emotional loss and impoverishment that accompanies the transition into adulthood (6). French psychoanalyst Serge Leclaire explains that Freud's child majesty, a figure he renames the "wonderful child," is "first of all the nostalgic gaze of the mother who made him into an object of extreme magnificence akin to the Child Jesus majesty, a light and jewel radiating forth absolute power" (2–3). This idealization neatly complements Damien's desire to be the good boy through his particular occupation as a priest (indicated not merely by his placement of the collar next to his sentimental childhood mementos but also by the collar being snatched away when he visits his mother in the hospital). Leclaire has given an extensive and forceful reading of Freud's "child majesty" scenario, emphasizing an oppressive or terrifying weight to this representation and the subject's need to "murder" that image to achieve full selfhood—what he calls the fantasy of "a child is being killed." For Leclaire, the murder of this first version of oneself, that "strange original image in which everyone's birth is inscribed" (2), is the most primal and unsettling of all fantasies. However, the death of the child within must occur, and repeatedly so (the act can never be finalized). Refusal of the nostalgic self-image of the wonderful child is the sole precursor to autonomous selfhood. It allows one to feel as if one is moving forward and not merely trapped in the preordained expectations of others. Through the death of the child, the subject no longer lives in the shadow of his or her cultural and familial replica. It is this nostalgic child that *The Exorcist* places in intense jeopardy. Fear for this child's endangerment takes place alongside—and as a monstrous expression of—Damien's inability to relinquish the same romanticized image. In Regan's seemingly acute relevance to him, the priest sees reflected the wonderful image of himself that he has atrociously sullied.

## "Come into me . . ."

Toward *The Exorcist*'s conclusion, in a scene included only in the 2000 director's cut ("The Version You've Never Seen"), Fathers Merrin and Karras sit hunched and dejected at different spots on the staircase we have traversed many times to behold the horrors of Regan's subzero bedroom upstairs. They face opposite directions, cast apart by the seemingly unceasing trauma of the event. Damien slowly questions his senior, although with a rhetorical lilt, as if pursuing an answer he knows he will not get: "Why this girl? It doesn't make sense." The senior father cannot answer with certainty, but has something telling to share. "I think the point is to make us despair. . . . To see ourselves as animal and ugly. . . . To reject the possibility that God could love us." Damien's face is held in tight close-up as he contemplates Merrin's response, his eyes contemplatively averted. The ailing Merrin excuses himself, moving to the bathroom to take his medication, and again Damien ventures upstairs toward Regan's room. Inside he sees not Regan but his mother again, clad in hospital whites in the center of the bed, her face chalk white around eyes cavernously black and unblinking.

As Damien moves around the bed, the hallucination terminates and Regan is restored. He dabs her forehead, helping her as he would have liked to help his bedridden mother, to redeem himself in that deep and unwavering gaze. Yet this child, scarred and putrid as she is, is also precisely as "animal" and "ugly" as Damien feels himself to be. Then Regan speaks in his mother's voice, restoring all his torment: "Dimi, *why you do this to me?* . . . Please, Dimi, I'm afraid." As Damien comes apart, unable to follow Merrin's previous instruction to ignore the demon's taunts, the senior priest intervenes, banishing him from the room. To the film's conclusion, Damien is unable to prevent seeing himself as animal and ugly, to disconnect his self-image from his mother's damning gaze.

Leclaire writes that the wonderful child figure "fully deserves to be called *infans*," the Latin word for child that means literally one who does not speak. Merrin's commanding prayer rituals outline a new role for Damien ("The response please, Damien"), allowing him to speak in a new and pressing persona. The rituals construct an identity for him, offering him a version of himself removed from his totalizing preoccupation with his mother. However, this becomes once again an expectation of which Damien feels he has fallen short when he is sent from the room like a disappointing child. When he reenters the room to find the older priest dead, he is again battered with the weight of having disappointed a "parent." Attempting to revive Merrin, Damien thumps upon his chest with surprising force, his trauma infused with the same aggression that roiled beneath his ordeal with his mother.

As Damien continues to plead with the dead Merrin to revive, Regan sits mesmerized, leaning limply against the bedpost. Then she draws her hands to her mouth and emits a childish snigger. But this particular giggle is not in the demon's voice (for the film has easily and effectively distinguished the two beings acoustically throughout). It is in the voice of any typically sniggering twelve-year-old kid. This child's laughter, this burst of infantile delight, in fact mirrors Regan's giggling earlier in the film as her mother chases her round the house and before she is possessed. Enraged at the sound, Damien throws himself toward her, hauls her onto the ground, and begins punching. Here, the attack on the "wonderful child," who is oppressive in her innocence, is both present and inadmissible. The film immediately defers the anxiety of "a child being killed" by overstating the demon's harsh masculinity: the giggle is replaced by a surly bellow, and Damien's body blocks our view of the child as he shouts at her, "You son of a bitch!" (this phrasing still managing to insinuate that he is attacking the child of his mother, the phantasmic image of her maternal desire). "Take me! Come into me!" Damien yells at the girl/demon in frustration, an offer the demon embraces as Damien throws himself from the upstairs window, annihilating the demonic threat and himself in a gesture of Christlike sacrifice. In his invitation to the demon, however, one might also see Damien's despairing admission of the demon's presence where it was all along:

within him, in the "atrocious" child of his self-conception. On the path outside, a fellow priest, Father Dyer (William O'Malley), helps the dying Damien to make a final confession, thereby reintegrating him into a narrative of belonging. However, in his suicide we see the terminus of his harrowing desperation to come to grips with the wonderful child (outside and inside himself). "The logic behind suicide," Leclaire suggests,

> derives from a perfect syllogism: in order to live, I must kill "myself"; or else, I don't really feel alive (this is no life!). . . . If we could only clear up . . . the confusion underlying the truth of the first statement—in order to live I must kill the tyrannical representation of the *infans* within me—then another logic would appear. (4)

Reencumbered by his failure to fulfill the persona laid out by the paternal Merrin, Damien is finally unable to disambiguate his identity. His inability to imagine himself outside his first, most intimate, and most sacred self-image means that the murder of the tyrannical child can only be conceived and enacted as total self-immolation.

## Conclusion

Religious horror films featuring child villains routinely affirm and remystify the "majesty" attributed to the child by dominant ideology, imbuing the culturally constructed child with supernatural significance. In *Bless the Child* (2000), a young girl possesses mysterious powers that ensure she is pursued by cultists trying to bring about a reign of evil. This child-as-battleground scenario is symptomatic of children's transmissive power in any society, its role in maintaining (and potentially upsetting) dominant ideologies. However, these fantasized scenarios also work to conceal both ideology and its transmission. The child is depicted not as a subject of cultural forces but as carrier of a kind of innate germ of all that is true, good, and natural, all that is angelically (or demonically) "beyond ideology." I have indicated at several points in this book that the cultural obsession with the innocent, vulnerable child means that children who fall outside that definition are construed as monstrous—as explosively and totally Other. In *The Exorcist*, however, this process is turned terrorizingly inward for the adult Damien. Feeling himself to have slipped from his mother's esteem, he can be only demonic. The priest is held hostage by a past version of himself, by a familial projection of innocence that is ultimately a construction of the wonderful child within his very soul (Leclaire writes that this representative forms in

the subject "what . . . is most secret, indeed sacred . . ." [10]). Having
lost his mother's adoration, he has also lost his faith and the possibility
that God could love him. Julia Kristeva suggests that the child and the
adolescent in literature are both "mythic figure[s] that the imaginary,
and of course, the theoretical imaginary, [give] us in order to distance
us from certain of our faults—cleavages, denials, or simply desires?—by
reifying them in the form of someone who has not yet grown up" (8).
In *The Exorcist*, precisely such a disavowal is served by the dramatic and
harrowing child-in-danger, by Damien's refusal to let go of the darling
young fellow he once was and continues to strive to be. In his character
we see a terrifying depiction of the power of definitions of childhood to
colonize our most intimate selves.

Regan survives the film, of course, to demonstrate to us the innocent
child restored. Her bruises remind us of her preciousness and enhance
her vulnerability, yet crucially (remembering nothing) she is psychologically uncontaminated by her ordeal. As moving as her reappearance may
be in its confirmation of her natural lovability, it is within the force of this
same image that the story's true demon lurks—the demon of children's
"majesty," who lives on, undetected.

# 8

## All Fun and Games till Someone Gets Hurt

### Hating Children's Culture

CHILDREN'S CULTURE IS A MINEFIELD in the horror film. "Let's play hide and go seek," cheeps the zombie-toddler of *Pet Sematary* (1989), prompting the wary old neighbor to go upstairs, where he will have his Achilles tendon sawed through with a scalpel. Henry (Macaulay Culkin) hurls his younger sister onto the thin ice of a frozen lake in *The Good Son* (1993) under the pretense of a jubilant skating escapade gone wrong. Hide-and-seek becomes a matter of life and death in the same film as the boy stalks through the house for his hapless sibling. "What do you think this is, a game?" he sneers balefully to the cousin (Elijah Wood) who leaps to the girl's defense. When the mutant baby of *It's Alive* hides in a preschool classroom, it transforms the environment (with its rows of grinning plush toys and building blocks shot from extreme low-angles) into a landscape as alien and unknowable as that of any intergalactic thriller. "Trick or treat" chimes a chorus of children's voices in the opening to John Carpenter's *Halloween* (1978) just minutes before the clown-suited child overpowers his sister with a kitchen knife. Even before *Halloween* made child's play into something deadly serious, Italian director Dario Argento's influential 1975 slasher *Deep Red* (*Profondo rosso*) had incorporated the symbolism of children's culture—dolls, drawings, songs—into a carnivalesque display of ruthless aggression that

131

excised it from the comfortable precincts of the familial home. Among the precursors to modern horrified visions of kid culture, we can count Fritz Lang's *M* (1931), in which, as a part of their playground rituals, children sing a song about the murdering child-molester at large: "Just you wait a little while, the nasty man in black will come / With his little chopper, he will chop you up!" So unsettling to the adults who over-hear it from nearby apartments, their tune superficially demonstrates the children's worrisome obliviousness to their own vulnerability. They have imagined the victimization of children such as themselves (a victimization of which the particular, gruesome details have no doubt been concealed from them) as a game. What's more, their song is used to "pick out" children from the group in perverse mimicry of the murderer's special selection of his prey. However, it also bespeaks the children's possession of a troubling folk knowledge of the killer, who, the film clearly points out, has left for his adult pursuers no clue to his identity. The same device is used in Wes Craven's *Nightmare on Elm Street* (1984), in which skipping children chant "One, two, Freddy's coming for you . . ." in reference to blade-fingered child killer Freddy Krueger (Robert Englund). It is thanks to *Child's Play*, however, that the apparently harmless and familiar world of the child has become as recognizable a figure in the cultural pantheon of fright as any serial killer, sewer mutant, or gelatinous visitor from

Figure 8.1. Chucky, the possessed children's doll, viciously attacks the parent who procured him (Catherine Hicks, out of frame) in Tom Holland's *Child's Play* (United Artists, 1988). Digital frame enlargement.

beyond. Here, a high-tech children's doll whose acquisition is demanded by a six-year-old and pursued by his hard-up single mother wreaks more than mere financial havoc after having been magically possessed by the spirit of a dead serial killer.

Horror's proclivity for child villains frequently transforms children's culture through mere association, making childish fun ironically synonymous with adult fear. However, children's culture has itself been used to evoke the nervous difference between adults and children and the violent usurpation of adult power. Beginning with a focus on the decontextualized displays of *Deep Red* and tracing its warped scattering of children's paraphernalia to the implied presence of the child as an undesirable, active subject rather than the passive subject of ideology impressed upon it by adults, we can move on to a consideration of the doll with reference to *Child's Play*, which (with a little help from a cavalcade of sequels) endures as the most famous evil toy film. Mannequins have a long history in the horror film, where they often appear in tandem with scheming ventriloquists, as in films like *The Great Gabbo* (1929), *Dead of Night* (1945), *Devil Doll* (1964), and *Lisa and the Devil* (1973), although the evil doll's role as a part of the iconography of childhood is more recent. *Dolls* (1987), in which a horde of pint-sized automata terrorize the houseguests of an elderly doll maker and his wife, openly associates its little terrors with the wondrous emotional domain of the child. However, the terrible toys of *Dolls* (wooden dolls, grenadier guards, etc.) strike one as curiously outdated alongside the novel, talking and slop imbibing dolls of the 1980s. In fact, these lovingly crafted anachronisms clearly represent childhood as imagined by the adult, a nostalgic, romanticized, and fundamentally subordinate identity, even as they brutalize perceived opponents of that ideal (punk rock hussies, careerist mothers, and wimpy fathers). It was a year later with *Child's Play* that the doll became a motif for negotiating the anxious idea of an unknowable and uncontrollable child.

The subject of children's culture in the horror film, especially the doll, compels us to consider Freud's 1919 essay "The Uncanny," which directs attention to the fear of the living doll in E. T. A. Hoffmann's story "The Sand-Man." Pointing out that dolls are "rather closely connected with childhood life" (233), Freud suggests that children's games are marked by a lack of differentiation between the animate and inanimate through which dolls assume the same status as real people. While Freud suggests that "children have no fear of their dolls coming to life, they may even desire it" (233), the potential accuracy of this otherwise long-dismissed childish belief is what troubles the adult. While Freud's analysis remains too undeveloped and metaphorical to be particularly helpful (as theorists like Anneleen Masschelein have pointed out), it nevertheless highlights the value attached to an elevated, adult perspective of children's culture. The doll upsets the surety of the adult's power over the child, haunting us with a childhood perspective unframed by adult reason. In Freud's formulation, the living doll is a return of a never quite conquered infantile belief. The reemergence and *realization* of this repressed content threaten an otherwise normalized adult authority over children, including the containment and dismissal of children's perspectives. Similarly, we might suggest that adults' secret skepticism of the legitimacy and moral truth of their authority over children can only leave them haunted by fantasies of the child viewpoints they repress. In either case, the fear of the living child's doll comes to us as a paranoid demonization of children's perspectives and as a striking challenge to the adult-child hierarchy. More than just an emblem of the difference between adult and child perception, the doll in *Child's Play* represents oppositional desires fueled by changes to contemporary marketing. Deeply informed by a cultural climate that saw children being targeted as a consumer demographic with unprecedented proficiency, *Child's Play* uses the doll to dramatize adult frustration toward the consumer child and the financial strain that accompanies him.

## No Place Like Home:
## *Deep Red* and the Iconography of Childhood

Argento's *Deep Red* follows the search for the perpetrator of murders committed in a bloodily flamboyant style (one for which its director is celebrated). One of the most striking aspects of this flamboyance is that the crimes are accompanied by an array of artifacts that render the otherwise familiar world of the child uncannily alien. At several crime scenes, a bald plastic doll dangles from a rope. From an obscure corner of a room, an automated mannequin is inexplicably propelled—arms swinging, voice a shrill chuckle—toward a victim just prior to his slaughter. And the repetition of a jubilant nursery jingle overcomes the soundtrack prior to the majority of the murders. Additionally, the investigator protagonist (David Hemmings) receives advice from a girl who maims lizards for fun, leading him to a macabre children's drawing of a wounded man alongside a knife-brandishing child. This estranged presentation of the signifiers of childhood is complemented by the film's Freudian overtones, which recall the psychoanalytic challenge to popular understandings of childhood as a space-time characterized by innocence and asexuality. The flashback with which the film commences, featuring a stabbing and what appears to be a partially hidden child who may or may not be the killer, suggests foundational trauma and repression, while the piano-playing protagonist hypothesizes that his choice of profession might be related to antipathy toward his father: "When I bang the keys I'm really bashing his teeth in."

But the imagery of childhood in *Deep Red* turns out to be a red herring. The killer, it turns out, is not a disturbed child after all, nor is she the partially obscured child of the opening scene. The film's psychiatrist attributes the childhood relics to the killer's need to meticulously frame the expression of her delirium, yet this vague speculation in no way accommodates the film's fascination with the unconventional placement of signifiers of childhood or their startling effect on the viewer. Instead, the childish additions linger like visual fetishes, remaining troublingly unframed. Maitland McDonagh refers to *Deep Red* as "the first of Argento's films to enter truly into the realm of Barthesian excess . . . displacing the emphasis of scene after scene from the narrative elements onto peculiar details that resonate way out of proportion to their overt importance" (12). While we cannot quite say what they mean (or perhaps *because* we cannot say what they mean), these decapitated or creepily automated dolls command far more of our interest than the narrative that contains them.

These evocative totems suggest the socializing ideologies urged upon the child by the adult through sanctioned play as well as the safety and nostalgia of childhood and its freedom from violence or sexuality. Injected into crime scenes, these comfortable, ideologically invested contrivances are drained of meaning. Shots linger on the blank expressions of the bald and glaringly plastic dolls, holding the viewer in contemplation of these powerful objects removed from the familial contexts they otherwise cozily complement and affirm. This jarring remystification of childhood creates within the film the suggestion of a world in which the nostalgic pleasure of the safest of places—the family home—simply does not exist. Viewer and protagonist both know they are dealing with a fundamental depravity from which not even comforting notions of home are a refuge.

Also uprooting the world of the child from its familiar ideological context in *Deep Red* is the use of children's music. A jubilant nursery melody is centralized in the perpetration of the crimes, its capricious refrain, nonsensical lyrics, and repetition gradually suggesting a mind trapped in neurotic involution. The opening scene, in which the sound of murder is drowned out by this tune, establishes a fundamental symbolic discord between sound and image sustained by subsequent murder scenes. This conflict is doubly emphasized by the confusion of diegetic and non-diegetic sound: Is the song "really" playing prior to the murders or merely a kind of perverse pit music? As it happens, the song is really (that is, diegetically) playing, the ostensibly knowing psychiatrist supposing it "the leitmotif of the crime." Drawing on the work of Gilles Deleuze and Félix Guattari, Patricia Pisters speaks of the musical refrain as "[creating] a stable center, a fragile point in the enormous black hole of chaos: a child comforts itself in the dark by singing softly a nursery rhyme" (189). She takes this further, indicating the relevance of Deleuze and Guattari's idea to music in cinema: "The refrain organizes around that stable point a calm 'pace' (rather than a form). This is what we call 'home.' Every household is an aurally marked territory. . . . Also, in cinema, music can have this function of creating a 'home' or at least a recognizable environment" (189). The stable, homely refrain of *Deep Red* is, however, troublingly mismatched. The accompaniment of the endless refrain by domestic brutality against adults radically debunks the security of the home (a rejection redoubled by the film's insistence on murders that take place in the comfort of the domestic sphere). Although the child is not the killer in *Deep Red*, the refrain denies the adult viewer's expectation of a sound-image synthesis that would imagine childhood culture according to stable ideological paradigms. The vicious stabbing of an adult with which the film commences, and through which the song is unwaveringly recited, reprocesses belonging into horrifying alienation, violently deconstructing the relationship between adult and child.

## Model Behavior: *Child's Play*

Of the alienating children's paraphernalia deployed in *Deep Red*, the child's doll has had by far the most successful career in the horror film, first taking center stage in *Dolls*, then in Child's Play (1988), which inspired a stream of sequels as well as imitations like *Puppet Master* (1989), *Silent Night, Deadly Night: The Toy Maker* (1991), *Demonic Toys* (1992), and *Dolly Dearest* (1992). With the release of *Child's Play*, however, the child's doll was elevated to the status of genre icon, a figure of the same cultural (if not physical) stature as Freddy Krueger, Jason Voorhees, or Michael Myers. The displaced and decolonized view of children's culture presented in *Deep Red* is considerably amplified in *Child's Play* through detailed and powerful reference to a contemporary climate of children's consumerism. Marketing and consumer culture commentator Juliet B. Schor points out that "the 1980s brought major changes in children's advertising. Companies began to see more potential in selling to kids. . . . Kraft started targeting kids for cheese, pasta, Jell-O, and pudding, in addition to longstanding child foods such as snacks and cereals" (41). While children may not have literally managed or generated family finances, the specific targeting of their desires positioned the child as an active force in consumption. Robert Bocock highlights the way in which consumption increasingly spoke directly to the desires of children, normalizing habits of consumption as a pathway to symbolic belonging:

> Consumption has emerged as a fundamental part of the process by which infants enter western capitalist cultures and their symbolic systems of meanings. Foods, drinks, toys, clothes and television are part of the early experiences of consumption of young children in western societies. Infants and children are being socialised into being consumers during the very early stages of development. (85)

Throughout the 1980s, understandings of childhood were increasingly mediated by advertising and consumer culture. *Child's Play* comments on these cultural shifts in intriguing and forceful detail, clearly positioning children's consumption within discourses of parental hardship and disempowerment.

The film commences with a standard police chase. An armed man in an overcoat (Brad Dourif) is legging it through the steam and bluish haze of a dark alley as a plainclothes police officer (Chris Sarandon) chases after him. They both bolt through the nighttime streets, rounding a few corners and firing a few shots until "the Strangler" is hit, his getaway car speeds away from him, and he seeks refuge in a closed toy store. The cop follows him inside and, after ducking and weaving among aisles of toys, manages to shoot the killer again. Cornered and dying, the Strangler promises revenge against both his accomplice and pursuer before hurling himself into a wall of boxes containing newfangled "Good Guy" dolls. Tearing one from the box, he pronounces an occult incantation to transfer his spirit to the toy before lightning strikes the store and the man himself is killed. Single mother Karen Barclay (Catherine Hicks) later purchases the much-in-demand but expensive doll (personalized "Chucky") from a homeless man, presenting it as a birthday treat for her young son, Andy (Alex Vincent). Before long, however, the toy reveals itself as a living, swearing, and deliriously homicidal miniature of the Strangler.

What is perhaps most immediately striking about *Child's Play* is the injection of children's culture into the gritty aesthetic of the police procedural. The brightness of the toy store in the film's opening scene presents a striking contrast to the industrial debris, rain-slicked streets, and rising steam of the city surrounding it. The neon glow of the Playland signage offers consumer comforts that few in such a degraded place can actually afford and suggests a wondrous fairyland location that exposes the adult's participation in definitions of family based on consumption. As the police officer pursues the Strangler into the store, the transition to a conspicuously low-angle point-of-view shot just a few feet above the ground denies the viewer visual control over the environment. The toy store is transformed from an idealistically light-hearted domain exempt from the grubby dealings of the city. And the adult spectator, forced to see through the imagined eyes of a child, is demoted to an inferior in the dream world of the infant. The fantastical toy store, over which the adult presumes dominance both financial and ideological, becomes an unpredictable environment where the adult is treated like a child.

During the pursuit inside the toy store, the film replaces the usual location props and sights of the police shoot-out—alleyway corners, trash cans, parked cars—with dimly lit shelves of children's paraphernalia. Mike the cop peeks, gun in hand, from behind a row of Power Play Hockey and Princess Power toys. As he threatens ultimate revenge, Ray the Strangler is framed conspicuously in front of a pink cellophane advertise-ment for Barbie Rockers, an odd choice of backdrop for the dying oaths of a madman killer. As in *Deep Red*, the positioning of children's culture in *Child's Play* displaces domestic familiarity and becomes a teasing denial of safety and the innocently simple world fabricated for children by adults. *Child's Play*, however, intimately connects this reversal of power with children's consumer desires, copiously illustrating a contemporary proliferation of children's commercial culture and the parental anxiety to which it gives rise. Schor points out that just as children were increas-ingly targeted as a profitable consumer demographic during the 1980s, parents became more willing to purchase the products they requested. The 1980s, she notes, "witnessed the dramatic upsurge in kids' influence power. There were fewer of what marketers called the 'authoritarian mom.' . . . Instead, 1980s mothers were more likely to be permissive or ambivalent moms, willing to buy the products on offer" (42). The scene that follows the toy store explosion presents a striking depiction of the escalation of children's consumerism through television and concludes by demonstrating tension between ambivalent parent and kid consumer. A dissolve from the jubilant features of a still-intact Chucky doll to a multicolored "happy birthday" banner resembling the toy store signage associates gifted toys with the danger of the film's opening scene. This threatening dimension to children's culture is underscored when the cam-era tilts gradually downward to identify a large, unopened present. The shot continues, panning slowly to take in a small living room overloaded with merchandise: an inflatable object upended behind the lounge suite on which there are a figurine, several toy trucks, a model airplane, and an abandoned, half-read comic. The room is empty but filled with the sound of the television switched to a cartoon program called *Good Guys*, the merchandise for which we have just exhaustively observed. We then see a shot from the squat perspective of the television itself as a young boy, Andy, apparently alerted by the show's distinctive jingle, swings around the kitchen bench and drops into the frame—the immediacy of his appearance and his insertion of himself into the shot conveying his apparently Pavlovian devotion to this program.

Andy's excitement is short lived. The episode is about a lonely boy joined by one of the Good Guys characters, who offers to be his "friend to the end." "I saw this one," he complains. The disappointment of his response highlights the ease with which genuine excitement and identification had just been fabricated by the television. Newly six years old and clad in Good Guys pajamas, Andy is up early making breakfast. Abandoning his bowl of Good Guys cereal under its avalanche of sugar, he again rushes into the living room to see an advertisement for the new Good Guys dolls of the film's opening scene. This time Andy is agog. The advertisement's instruction to "Remember to tell mom and dad, you want a Good Guy!" prefigures the viewer's knowledge that Andy's family doesn't have a dad, amplifying the difficulty and strain involved in purchasing the products he desires.

In this scene, the film suggests an almost endless propagation of interrelated children's consumer products, constructing an image of children's consumerism that, while outwardly innocent, signifies parental hardship, particularly for lower- or single-income families like the Barclays. Andy then finishes cooking breakfast and carries it to his sleeping mother in an attempt to get his birthday started. The knowing glance he gives a rectangular parcel along the way indicates his expectation of one of the marvelous dolls.

Not only do the gifts that Karen presents fall short of Andy's hopes, but they also explicitly indicate the financial pressure she is under. She realizes that he does not want "boring old clothes," although they comprise basic necessities she is under pressure to provide. She heralds her final gift as something of an indulgence, although still, despite the boy's anticipation, this isn't the doll he wanted, but a Good Guys tool set. The adult viewer's relief (whew!—this is not the bewitched doll of the film's opening scene) counters the child's obvious disappointment. The suggestion that a Good Guys tool set is the kind of gift with which Andy would presumably be happy (had he not recently seen the advertisement for a newer product) illustrates Baudrillard's assertion that "*there are no limits to consumption*" by suggesting that this child ultimately cannot be satisfied. "If it was that which it is naively taken to be," Baudrillard writes, "an absorption, a devouring, then we should achieve satisfaction"

(24). Moreover, this delusion is one to which children are particularly susceptible.

The scene ends in disappointment, leaving open the tension between Andy's desires and his mother's financial strain. The tone of Karen's voice hardens as the anxious discourse of financial struggle intrudes upon childhood wonder:

ANDY: "I want a Good Guy to go with it."

KAREN: "I know you do, Andy—but I didn't know about it in time this month to save up for it."

The debut of the evil doll Chucky is prefigured, then, by a view of children's commercial culture as not merely a realm of wonder and excitement but also an insidious and powerful exploiter of childhood excitement, indifferently propagating financial hardship and familial disconnection. For Andy, Chucky may represent identification and friendship, but for single mother Karen, who works as a department store clerk, he is already a villain.

The Good Guys dolls were a sinister presence in the film's opening scene before the murderer fixated on one. The title insert is placed in front of the large stack of the toys, their very commodification clearly inscribed with menace. The chilling laugh of the electric Chucky doll is even incorporated into the *Good Guys* show itself, bespeaking the latent villainy of its exhortations to consume. Chucky himself appears to be a higher-tech version of Playskool's popular 1985 "My Buddy" boys' doll. However, in a mini-documentary attached to one of the later *Child's Play* films, "Conceiving the *Seed of Chucky*" (2005), writer Don Mancini admits that Chucky was in fact modeled with the ubiquitous Cabbage Patch Kids dolls in mind. The popularity and exacting price of these dolls, as well as the pressure families were put under to ensure their child was satisfied with one, certainly urges their comparison with the Chucky doll. Claudia Mitchell and Jacqueline Reid-Walsh mention the awareness of financial hardship wrapped up in childhood memories of the Cabbage Patch Kid, relaying a woman's recollection of her distress upon realizing her parents had bought her one of the cheaper Cabbage Patch knockoffs (61). Karen, of course, gets one of the dolls for Andy after all, purchasing "Chucky" from a vagrant at a severe discount. Once she does so, she takes some time to inspect the box the doll came in. Its "He wants *you* for a best friend" slogan has both exploitative and militaristic connotations: children's consumption as recruitment. Her cynicism toward manipulative marketing techniques is demonstrated when she reads the slogan for herself: " 'He wants you for a best friend' . . . Yeah, right." A scene in which she returns to the backstreet location where she bought the doll in search of the homeless peddler offers a striking portrait of the looming specter of abject poverty, the unrecognized world to which she must subject herself in pursuit of her child's consumer comforts.

Inhabited by the spirit of the murderer, Chucky secretly comes alive at will, walloping the family's babysitter out of an upstairs window, getting even with the Strangler's treacherous accomplice, and finally turning on little Andy himself. The idea of the magical living doll invites tension between Andy and his mother over the boy's insistence that Chucky is "alive." The horrifying reality of this assertion stands as a metaphor for the potency of her son's advertising-oriented imagination and attributes a demonic or occult undercurrent to children's consumerism. The film demonstrates the way advertising taps into the desires of children and also imagines the child as troublingly synonymous with (and as blameworthy as) the marketing programs designed to capitalize on and exploit those desires. In fact, *Child's Play* openly encourages the viewer to compare Chucky and Andy. They are of similar size and wear matching multicolor Good Guys clothing. These associations are made explicit when Andy is suspected of murdering the babysitter. While the boy himself is an idealized, untouchably "cute" child who loves his mother, the evil doll becomes a stand-in toward whom parental hatred and anxiety may be uncontroversially directed. Chucky eventually tracks down his voodoo instructor (Raymond Oliver), from whom he seeks a solution to his condition. However, when his mentor refuses, Chucky produces a doll-sized reproduction of the man before snapping its leg in a gesture that (movie lore has long warned us) signifies the breaking of the actual individual's leg. This scene draws attention to dolls as facsimiles, implicitly raising the question of whom Chucky is a representation. In this way, *Child's Play* effectively splits the child in two. We can assure ourselves that we still do love kids while hating their culture and labeling their emotional desires a kind of chaotic, occult force. The distended special-effects ritual with which the film concludes, in which Chucky is first shot, then set on fire, then shot again, then decapitated and dismembered, emphasizes the adult's obsessive need for this doll (and all of children's unaffordable consumer items) to be defaced, burned as an effigy of the child's uncontrolled longings. However, it is also an effigy that connotes cathartic violence to the child's own body.

After Chucky's exhaustingly protracted demise, Andy is the last to leave the room, remaining fixated on the burned doll. The film's very conclusion, a freeze-frame of the boy being led by the hand from the room and looking back at the motionless doll through the door left ajar, not only insinuates a sequel (the door "left open") but also suggests disappointment and reluctance on the part of the boy. The "friend" promised in the television advertisements has been destroyed. The possibility that Chucky might come back to life once again is a direct extension of the film's haunting failure to address the child's emotional satisfaction and the automatic and powerful reprocessing of his desire into anxiety. As long as children still have emotional needs and Andy still longs for that "friend to the end," there remains the possibility of further terror.

 Child's Play's demonic depiction of children's consumerism has continued to thrive in the horror film. In Maria Lease's film Dolly Dearest, which features a mélange of themes pilfered from The Omen, The Exorcist, and Child's Play, a doll imbued with the evil spirit of a lost civilization being excavated nearby attempts to possess the young daughter of an American businessman and his wife. The doll is the ultimate bad influence, causing the girl to become morose and withdrawn, while her vulnerability to its power is linked with children's affection for material comforts, effecting an overlap that, as in Child's Play, implicitly villainizes the child. As the film's title suggests, the central concern of Dolly Dearest is the child's attachment to its material possessions, the idea that children might become "possessed" by their toys: "I've a daughter at home who's being controlled by a fucking doll!" screams Denise Crosby in one scene. "Now you tell me what the hell that is!" In Dolly Dearest, as in Child's Play, the forces of commodity capitalism are the real demon, exploiting children's desires for friendship and emotional engagement.

## Conclusion

The consumer child has continued to be the subject of barely disguised hatred in popular film, reinforcing the power of the cultural frustrations that underlie Child's Play. In Babe (1995), the Hoggett farm is visited by Mrs. Hoggett's daughter (Zoe Burton) and her husband (Paul Goddard), who bring with them from the city their two brats gorged on a modern consumer culture from which the farm is conspicuously removed. Upon being gifted an extravagant handmade dollhouse, the granddaughter (Brittany Byrnes) unwraps her present in a gluttonous frenzy before erupting in tears and wailing, to the viewer's disgust, "It's the wrong one—I want the house I saw on the television!" In Brian Levant's Christmas comedy Jingle All The Way (1996), Howard Langston (Arnold Schwarzenegger) asks his son what he would like for Christmas before having the entire commercial for newfangled "Turboman" action figures parroted back at him, followed by the assurance that anyone who doesn't get one is "going to be a real loser." "Well, that definitely won't be you!" Howard replies, snatching the boy into an embrace as the score swells in loving endorsement of the family's communion through consumerism. But this of course sets up the problem that brings the story to life: Howard fears that his son's love will be retracted if he cannot get the consumer product he desires. Part of the fun of *Jingle All The Way* is certainly the child's bullying of a juggernaut of action cinema, with Schwarzenegger's tough-guy status additionally recalled when he roughs up two sarcastic store clerks and takes on an army of fake Santa Clauses. Implicit in the film's humor is the constant knowledge of the ease with which Schwarzenegger, an icon of cinema violence, could theoretically drop this "family friendly" façade of paternity and pulverize the demanding little twerp. Instead, the film offers us humorous surrogates—in one scene he punches to pieces a cardboard cutout of his son's hero.

The popular 1998 film *Small Soldiers* betrays similar frustrations toward kids' consumer desires. The fear underlying toys coming to life in this film is clearly that their child consumers will embrace their aggressive influence (an aggression cynically acknowledged and marketed by the toys' producers). The movie's villainous rogue toys, a hypermilitarized line called the "Commando Elite," extend the connotations of recruitment implicit in *Child's Play* to link the child's consumerism with induction into a fascist ideal. The answer to this problem, however, is still more violence. The final scene makes the aggressive destruction of the toys and the protection of the besieged home a family affair—even mom joins in. Smashing and burning these symbols of children's desire is just the therapeutic release the adult deserves. In the *Harry Potter* franchise, the viewer delights in the various misfortunes that befall tyrannical child consumer Dudley Dursley (Harry Melling), whom orphan Harry (Daniel Radcliffe) in *The Sorcerer's Stone* (2001) is forced to both tolerate and degradingly serve. The scene of Dudley's birthday demonstrates that his consumer desire is characterized not by real enjoyment of consumer products but by insistence that his parents' finances have been satisfactorily strained in their acquisition: prior to unwrapping a single present, he rages over their number—a mere thirty-six compared with the previous year's thirty-eight. When bushy half-giant Hagrid (Robbie Coltrane) hexes the whiney brat with a swine's tail, we gleefully assent to the humiliating exposure of his otherwise unchecked piggery. However, these commercial insecurities have been expressed with the most force in horror cinema. In *Child's Play*, the division between adult and child is memorably enhanced through the construction of children's consumer desire as ruinous demand. It remains certainly the most aggressive expression of anxiety toward children's consumerism in mainstream cinema.

Jane Kenway and Elizabeth Bullen point out the predatory, cynical exploitation that exists within the advertising industry, citing advertising agency president Nancy Shalek's feeling that "[a]dvertising at its best is making people feel that without their product, you're a loser. Kids are very sensitive to that. . . . You open up emotional vulnerabilities [which is] very easy to do with kids because they're the most emotionally vulnerable" (210). However, Kenway and Bullen also observe that in addition to helping construct children's desires, children's commercial culture also helps us to understand them. As Schor points out, in their research

> [m]arketers . . . concur that kids want love. . . . Common strategies for conveying love are the use of stuffed animals, sweet-looking dolls, and objects with rounded surfaces. Child development experts, brain scientists, and psychologists have helped marketers translate the desire for love into concrete objects, shapes, music, and themes for ads. (46)

In *Child's Play*, however, we can see only the ruinous dimension of children's desires, their abbreviation and transformation by capitalism into an uncanny automaton that obscures the child's emotional needs. The doll, a signifier of the child's desire for love, has become a mystical force answerable only with violence and degradation.

9

## Too Close for Comfort

### Child Villainy and Pedophilic Desire
### in *Hard Candy* and *Orphan*

I NCREASINGLY IN WESTERN CULTURE, children are recognized by adults as potential objects of erotic attraction for other adults. The horror of this realization affects the way we see children presented onscreen: how they can or cannot be shown as well as how we permit ourselves to see them. The reality and power of this discomforting awareness of the child's possible eroticism might be illustrated through a number of filmic examples; here is one. In the conclusion to Jack Clayton's 1961 film *The Innocents*, the governess (Deborah Kerr) chases her increasingly troublesome ward, Miles (Martin Stephens), into the manor courtyard, convinced that he has been possessed by the spirit of Quint, the estate's former and lascivious valet. Despite having died after a drunken slip one night prior to the governess's arrival, Quint has taken to appearing around the property in pursuit (or so the governess imagines) of the children. The trouble, famously, is that the governess is the only one to have seen the ectoplasmic letch. Upon capturing Miles, she urges the boy to confess his knowledge of the phantom. Miles admits nothing, even after the ghost appears in plain view atop a nearby stone platform. With an enigmatic wave of the hand, the spook vanishes (perhaps he was never there at all) and the boy falls to the ground. The governess is relieved, believing him safe from Quint's corrupting influence. Miles, however, is

45

dead, killed in a metaphoric exchange: his holy innocence was traded for the governess's recognition of her own latent sexuality. She cries out, and then it happens: with the sound of birds chirping energetically in the background, the thirtysomething Kerr plants an unsettlingly prolonged kiss on the mouth of child actor Stephens.

There is no doubt that this climax was at least awkward in 1961, but it could not possibly have aspired to the discomfort it provokes in the modern viewer. *The Innocents* is a weird film, doing relatively little to sort out the legendary ambiguity of Henry James's *The Turn of the Screw*, on which it is based—but it is not *that* weird: this final scene provides one of the most strikingly uncomfortable indications that the manner in which we conceptualize the child has changed. Now, more than at any other moment in Western culture, children's status as potential objects of sexual desire for adults is recognized as a problem. For the modern viewer, the Kerr-Stephens kiss is a veritable affright, and the idea of the child as an erotic object—of *pedophilia*—hangs over the scene like a pall.

As I have suggested, Miles of *The Innocents* is not positioned as a sexual object but signifies the lack of one. The film's romance or lack thereof is not with the child; he is a cipher through whom the governess imagines her own internal battle between innocence and sexuality being played out. In the world of the film, innocence is sexuality's opposite and the child is the former's beatified representative. After sexuality is acknowledged, the figure that has signified its repression is eliminated. From this perspective, the concluding kiss, however awkward and cultur-ally illegible, is hardly morally worrisome. The world today is a different place, though, and it seems highly unlikely that the scene would even be composed in this fashion if the film were remade. We might quickly juxtapose it with Jonathan Glazer's *Birth* (2004), in which Nicole Kidman plays a woman who believes a young boy is her dead husband reincar-nated. This film was greeted with controversy over a scene in which Nicole Kidman is depicted sharing a bath with her then ten-year-old costar Cameron Bright, albeit with no physical contact at all.

The question of children's sexual desirability is anxiously centralized in two films: David Slade's 2005 thriller *Hard Candy* and Jaume Collet-Serra's *Orphan* from 2009. *Hard Candy* knows very well that the world is a different place today and clearly intends to appeal to a viewer who is acutely aware of (perhaps even titillated by) the specter of pedophilia. After conversing with unsettling naiveté in an Internet chat room, four-teen-year-old Hayley Stark (Ellen Page) agrees to meet up with thirty-two-year-old Jeff (Patrick Wilson), a hipster slimeball who makes a living as a fashion photographer of underage girls and affects fandom of trendy electropop to impress her. With audience-provoking negligence, Hayley accompanies Jeff to his house, although he gets more than he bargained for when she drugs the predator and sets about terrorizing him, the film veritably daring us to sympathize with the pedophile. *Orphan's* treatment of the child villain is in many ways more conventional, yet this film bears a marked similarity to *Hard Candy* in its discomforting reference to pedophilia. Yuppie couple Kate and John Coleman (Vera Farmiga and Peter Sarsgaard), evidently dissatisfied with their existing children, set their heart on adopting Esther (Isabelle Fuhrman), a Russian girl living in a US orphanage. Esther's toxic upheaval of the Coleman family is most confrontingly expressed through her attempted seduction of her adoptive father toward the end of the film in a moment that, like *Hard Candy*, seeks to implicate the viewer in awkward pedophilic desires. Having consistently compromised John's relationship to his wife, especially in its sexual expression, Esther prepares herself as a sex object for her new father in a scene that plays on profound anxieties surrounding the boundaries between the Othered pedophile and the self. In both films, we can see the irrepressible awareness of children's potential identification as sex objects as well as a culturally panicked management of that knowledge—negations that leave pressing questions about pedophilia as a social problem unanswered.

## Naughty but Nice: *Hard Candy*

The fourteen-year-old Hayley Stark of *Hard Candy* has the apparent smarts to decline a drink from Jeff, the photographer whose clandestine chat-room flirtations have lured her back to his posh bungalow home. She chooses, however, to mix one herself, including one for her predator. Jeff awakens later the same day, having been drugged by his sassy would-be victim and neatly duct-taped to a chair. "Playtime," Hayley acidly informs him, "is over." Turning Jeff's home upside down, she eventually discovers a safe filled with child pornography, including a (non-nude) photograph of missing local teenager Donna Mauer. After a series of struggles, Jeff finds himself pantless and tied down, spread-eagled, on a large metal table as Hayley—a precocious medical enthusiast—prepares to castrate him "for the good of society." *Hard Candy* cost just a million dollars to produce but went on to make more than seven million dollars worldwide. The film had its Hollywood premiere in 2006 at the Arclight Cinemas in Los Angeles, where it grossed almost thirty thousand dollars per theater ("Creating Hard Candy"). It was also widely reviewed upon release, with noted English film critic and *Sight and Sound* regular Mark Kermode heaping praise on the film. Roger Ebert, granting it three and a half of four stars, referred to *Hard Candy* as an "impressive and effective" film that provokes "an undeniable fascination in the situation as it unfolds" and joined a chorus of rave reviews for Page's performance as the unlikely vigilante. While this film has hardly become a ubiquitous point of reference in the way of *The Bad Seed* (1956) or *The Exorcist* (1973), its success testifies to the appeal of its subject to the imagination of the cinema-going public and the acute relevance of representations of the child as an erotic object. Throughout this book I have devoted considerable attention to child villains whose evil is disturbingly pronounced; villains—such as Damien of *The Omen* (1976) or Rhoda of *The Bad Seed* (1956)—whom we have little choice but to despise. The child vigilante of *Hard Candy*, however, deliberately compromises the distinction between villain and protagonist, victim and villain. In what follows, I suggest that *Hard Candy* presents a child aggressor with whom we sympathize in order to push the ominous figure of the pedophile further from ourselves.

*Hard Candy* commences with an extreme close-up of a computer screen displaying an ongoing conversation between "lensman319" and "Thonggrrrl14," the former's avatar a picture of a camera, the latter's a naive love heart. It is a highly generic scenario (we might be watching a commercial for child protection) but one that, in this emphatically decontextualized form, functions as a shorthand way of constructing the viewer as parental. The trendily minimalist aesthetic of the chat applet draws attention to the participants and conversation content, provoking the suggestion that Thonggrrrl14 is indeed merely fourteen—and the inevitable, accompanying suspicion that the "lensman" is much older. The oblique angle shots of the screen here suggest knowledge snatched from the secretive world of the adolescent, relegating the viewer to the realm of the concerned spectator. The girl's use of a "drooling" emoticon—:)~~~—gives us momentary pause for translation, only to alienate the concerned adult with the openness of this sexual display. The secretarially proficient clack of the keyboard itself implies a vibrant life lived outside parental knowledge and an adolescent technological savvy that far exceeds attention to safety. With a fatal keystroke, the scene terminates to black: the viewer expects the worst.

In its portrayal of a standard child-safety nightmare, however, one of *Hard Candy*'s most interesting moves is to do away with the pedophile as wheezing trench-coated bogey. When Hayley travels to a café to meet her predator, the man who arrives is amiable, handsome, and stylishly dressed. Hayley's vulnerable "red riding hood" costume is denied a sufficiently wolfish counterpart. She comments that Jeff "doesn't really look like the kind of guy who has to meet girls on the Internet." For the remainder of this scene, Jeff is on the border, neither trustworthy nor too obviously villainous. Upon his arrival, he wipes a smear of chocolate

Figure 9.1. Wolf in sheep's clothing: the unexpectedly dashing predator, Jeff (Patrick Wilson), upon meeting his would-be love interest, the fourteen-year-old Hayley Stark (Ellen Page, out of frame) in David Slade's *Hard Candy* (Lionsgate, 2005). Digital frame enlargement.

from Hayley's lower lip and tastes it—a discomforting moment, but one that falls short of the outright predacity we expect, particularly given Hayley's refusal (caught by Jeff's unexpectedly dashing appearance) to play overtly the shy and shrinking innocent.

After purchasing a T-shirt for Hayley and asking her to try it on, Jeff seems to endure her coquetry with good humor and respects her privacy as she changes clothes. His dialogue in this scene is not nearly as sexualized as that of the film's opening conversation. Perhaps his Internet comments were inappropriate but ultimately unserious flirtation, underneath which is an actual respect of adult/child sexual boundaries? Hayley's suggestion that she accompany him back to his house is first greeted with reluctance, as he labels the idea "a little insane." This ambivalent characterization of Jeff, without the morally panicked hyperbole we might have expected, is fundamental to *Hard Candy*. We expect him to be sinister—and he does go some way toward fulfilling that expectation—but his representation also contains unassimilable moments of politeness, generosity, and respectfulness. Yet the more the film makes him a figure with whom we can identify, the more we are unsure, and the more worrying a figure he becomes.

The temptation of the viewer to identify with Jeff is uncomfortably underscored by the manner in which Hayley is framed, with a number of shot/reverse shots forcing us to imagine how Jeff sees her. James R. Kincaid suggests that what can metaphorically be termed cultural factories ("the ones that make meaning for us") are responsible for telling us both "what 'the child' is and what 'the erotic' is." He argues that "for the past two hundred years or so, they have confused us, have failed to distinguish the two categories, have allowed them dangerously to overlap" ("Producing Erotic Children" 247). *Hard Candy* deliberately emphasizes this overlap. The extreme close-up of a fork slowly cutting through a chocolate dessert with which the café scene commences positions Hayley as a delicacy herself. A medium close-up of her in profile depicts her enjoying the "childish" pleasure of eating the chocolate while emitting an unmistakably sexual moan. As Jeff approaches, an eyeline match singles out Hayley. As she turns, her face is shot in soft-focus that ensures freckles or blemishes fade into a virtuous white image of wide-eyed innocence. This halo of light is juxtaposed with the "childish" smear of chocolate on her parted lips, as the inability to accurately feed oneself suggests an eroticized infancy where reliance on adults is connected with sexual power.

Kincaid suggests that as far as the cinematic child is concerned, "desirable faces must be blank, washed out of color, eyes big and round and expressionless, hair blond or colorless altogether, waists, hips, feet, and minds small" (247). The presentation of Hayley in the film's opening scenes is of a girl washed with warm and placid yellow, wide-eyed, clear-skinned, and high-angled into supplication. Her face a shining canvas that offers nothing of its own character, Hayley represents the young girl as whatever we want her to be, flattering the viewer's empowered gaze.

While *Hard Candy* deliberately establishes the child as an erotic object, inviting a self-conscious and offensive rapport between the viewer

Figure 9.2. Eroticized infancy: moist-mouthed and wide-eyed, Hayley (Ellen Page) turns to greet her adult pursuer in *Hard Candy* (David Slade, Lionsgate, 2005). Digital frame enlargement.

and the suspected predator, the film's initial, urgent establishment of the viewer-as-parent means this voyeuristic gaze is always disturbingly conscious, providing a kind of embedded commentary that all the time reminds us we are watching "like a pedophile." For Kincaid, the pedophile "is our most important citizen, so long as he stays behind the tree or over in the next yard: without him we would have no agreeable explanation for the attractions of the empty child. We must have the deformed monster in order to assure us that our own profiles are proportionate" (*Child-Loving* 5). Yet in *Hard Candy* the profile of the viewer and the pedophile are rendered troublingly similar. Because of this, the film efficiently contaminates our sympathy for the victim and prevents us from questioning Hayley's later torture of him. Long before we have evidence that Jeff has actually molested anyone, our identification with Hayley is specifically designed to capitalize on the fear of identifying with the pedophile. Our identities are under question, and the film coerces the viewer into accepting the lurid tortures performed by its child antihero. The more we assent to Hayley's antagonism—and the more antagonistic she gets—the more we can keep Jeff at a decisive distance.

## Surgical Separation: The Viewer and the Pedophile

After Hayley drugs him, Jeff awakens with his suit jacket pulled over his head to resemble a black hood, objectifying him ridiculously in what seems a deliberate visual reference to the highly publicized Abu Ghraib prison photos of 2004. Now the style in which Hayley's face is shot is markedly deromanticized. Noirishly stark, metallic blue lighting complements a harder focus, bringing out pockets of shadow in her face; a bag under one eye underscores a stare of derision. Visual pleasure in looking at her is denied; gone is the persistent, sexualized, eager-to-please innocence of the film's earlier scenes. It is Jeff's turn to be looked at, a symbolic indication of this coming when Hayley ridicules the photographer's gaze by putting on his sports jacket and glasses to accuse him of pedophilia. These scenes invite us to hold the pedophile at a distance, separating his gaze from our own. When Hayley rifles through Jeff's apartment, we take voyeuristic interest in labeling him what we suspect him to be. If Jeff is indeed a pedophile, his whole house can apparently be taken as public property to be rummaged and exposed so that we can see exactly what he is and what we are not. This attempted viewer/predator separation climaxes with the film's castration scene. As Jeff lays seminaked on the operating table, the shot moves down his body, objectifying him. The scene asks viewers to renounce the pedophile with a vengeance or endure castration by proxy. As an act of literal desexualization, the castration of the pedophile doubles as a metaphor for the final divorce of the innocent from the erotic.

In a film like *Death Wish* (1974), the vigilante was undoubtedly intended as a sympathetic figure of back-to-basics moral sanity and public hope. *Hard Candy*, however, provokes more serious questions about the morality of its vigilante's actions. The film's focus on character interaction—its conspicuous deficit of music, its stark set pieces and almost real-time trajectory, like that of *12 Angry Men* (1957) or *High Noon* (1952)—suggest an uninterrupted and high-pressure emphasis on moral interrogation. It is a film that seems to be partly about viewer identification and works to subvert the viewer's expectation of a stable antagonist/ protagonist relationship. *Death Wish* commenced with a rape and murder of more-than-adequate brutality to sustain character and viewer outrage across the course of the film. *Hard Candy*, however, refuses until its very conclusion to disclose whether Jeff in fact murdered missing teenager Donna—or whether he even molested her. The film is overwhelmed by the question of whether Jeff's pedophilia alone is reason enough to throw his whole life overboard, given our devotion to the coveted and uncomplicated innocence of the child.

This moral emphasis, however, is undermined by the delight we are invited to take in Hayley's actions. Her playful wit urges the viewer to revel in her transgressions and constructs degradation of the pedophile as enjoyment. This response is encouraged not only by character dialogue (which we may or may not consider morally sanctioned). As Hayley takes a brief walk outside, a neighbor (Sandra Oh) snipping her roses in an adjacent backyard provides an amusingly civilized reminder of Hayley's impeding "cut": castration suddenly is made comical. The jig seems to be up when the same neighbor knocks on Jeff's door and Hayley suddenly transforms into a surprisingly inept liar. The interruption gives viewers pause to contemplate whether they do in fact want Jeff's punishment to continue. However, a witty reminder of Jeff's pedophilia—the woman is selling Girl Scout Cookies for her daughter—defuses anxiety and swings the momentum in favor of his prolonged torment. During the castration scene, a very sorry Jeff tearfully recalls for Hayley an incident in his childhood when his aunt threatened to burn him after she caught him playing a little too intimately with one of his cousins as she emerged from the bathtub, thereby suggesting that his desires might be rooted in childhood trauma. Yet Hayley ignores the story and presses forward, thereby dismissing any sympathy the story might have evoked in the viewer as absurdly naive: "What was that supposed to be?—some kind of magic key to explain why you are the way you are?" she sarcastically asks. "It doesn't." In this intriguing scene, the film deliberately engages with pedophilia as a complex social and psychological phenomenon to snappily dismiss such contemplation and press forward with the torment.

Toward its conclusion, *Hard Candy* becomes even more explicit about whom we ought to be cheering for. After the procedure, as Hayley showers, Jeff wiggles and squirms his way to escape and, glancing downward in fear at his still-numbed nether region, realizes that the castration has in fact been an elaborate ruse. Hayley had filmed the procedure using one of his cameras, projecting it through a television for him to watch in real time. Pressing eject on his VCR, though, Jeff discovers a surgical video of castration procedures designed to fool him into thinking he was viewing his own manhood's mutilation. When he grabs a kitchen knife, the film begins to stabilize into a traditional slasher. When Hayley evades him, sprinting outside, Jeff screams and plunges his knife over and over into the crotch area of a mounted photograph of a young girl: shame on the viewer who doubted he was every inch the scumbag. The knife here is reaffirmed as a traditional phallic symbol, and Jeff's threat to Hayley, "I'll make it good for you, I promise," openly connects the knife with sexual attack. With this twist, *Hard Candy*'s characters slip into easily recognizable killer and victim roles, and viewers are conveniently permitted to dismiss much of the moral questioning that has otherwise prevented their full enjoyment of Jeff's torment. Feeling freshly empowered by his escape, Jeff acknowledges his pedophilia without shame, further disposing of any moral ambivalence the viewer might have harbored. A successful separation has been performed. The viewer is granted license to fully abandon Jeff, and the decisiveness of his renewed characterization obscures the damage willfully done before the evidence was in.

## Adult Irresponsibility, or the Child with No Name

"Does my face lie?" Hayley asks upon meeting Jeff. It does, and in more ways than one. This emphasis on Hayley's physical vulnerability (she is crushed violently against a wall in one scene) and the adult concern with which we are inclined to view her obscures the suspicion that, despite Page's playful performance, there is really little that is "childlike" about what we are watching. Early in the film, after being surprised at her own inability to find *any* kind of pornography in Jeff's home, Hayley exhibits none of the disgust toward what she was looking for that we might have expected in a girl her age. Her assessment that "[i]t's just the way [males] are brought up" has a retrospective, even sociologically informed ring to it, a confident adult knowingness in turn derided by Jeff's sarcastic remark, "You've done studies on this?" Later, she might be an outraged parent when she castigates Jeff for encouraging her flirtation:

"Just because a girl knows how to imitate a woman does not mean she's ready to do what a woman does!" As she composes an e-mail to Jeff's ex-girlfriend, tipping her off to his pedophilia, she deliberately makes her prose "as innocent and moronic as possible," thus showcasing her ability to adopt childhood as a specious persona. *Hard Candy*'s child-as-vigilante is a performance for the adult viewer. The child aggressor, despite being caught up in the discourses of the child that make us fear for her well-being, is an adult surrogate. A surrogate, yet not an adult: a concoction that renders Jeff's torture a less overtly moralistic pleasure than it would be were it perpetrated by an adult.

The film's final scene frees us from the lurid, claustrophobic décor of the house interior. Jeff having escaped and Hayley having sprinted outside, we see a shot of Jeff's former lover driving through the hills leading to his house. The new emphasis on natural landscape complements the characters' final "showdown" on the roof. This subtle Western reference, with the characters framed against a late-afternoon landscape that could easily be the mountains of Wyoming or Dakota (yet with rocky outcrops that evoke Monument Valley), invokes a cultural form that urges the viewer to choose sides and understand the film's overdetermined morality as emblematic confrontation. In fact, the generic trope with which the film concludes is the "Man with No Name," the figure inaugurated with the spaghetti Westerns of Sergio Leone, played by Charles Bronson and (most often and iconically) Clint Eastwood.[1] After the extent of Hayley's lying to Jeff suggests that even her name is probably fictitious, he barks at her in frustration, "Who are you?!" Her reply, "Every little girl you ever watched, touched, hurt, screwed, killed," renders her a pint-sized echo of "Harmonica" (Bronson) in Leone's *Once Upon a Time in The West* (1968) as he pursues sadistic gun for hire Frank (Henry Fonda) while assuming the names of Frank's victims. The film's final reference to this stock character constructs the vigilante child as someone whose intense self-possession lets us admire her but, as with the Man with No Name, feel no sense of "social responsibility" for her ultimately amoral behavior.

*Hard Candy*'s child offers viewers a way out, ultimately absolving them of any guilt in the questionable ferocity of their surrogate's brand of justice. Hayley may not be the pedophilic fantasy that Jeff desires, but she is a figure of adult fantasy nevertheless, and in these final scenes she recedes into a kind of moral vacuum. As an antagonist and as a child, Hayley may ultimately earn our disapproval, but this shift toward indifference represses the pleasure implied in her behavior. In his discussion of *The Omen*, William Paul speaks briefly of the "terrible fun" (328) of seeing the child villain's final smirk into the camera after having outlived his father. This "fun" is tied up with the idea of the horror film as ultimately unserious. *Hard Candy* invites us to find a very similar fun in Hayley's transgressions, as her irreverent wit suggests. She is the child who, for her ultimate harmlessness, is temporarily granted license to act out our own fantasies with guiltless abandon. The film offers us a chance to retain our parental control by outwardly disapproving of her actions. However, this belies our identification with her and the energy put into labeling and destroying the pedophile for our peace of mind. Jeff's occupation, of course, implicates him in the fashion industry as a "culture factory" of child eroticism. *Hard Candy* invites us to exorcize a pervasive cultural problem through the defeat of a personified single villain. The definition of the pedophile at which the film finally arrives is an Other of the most satanically straightforward variety, the very simplicity of his evil implying that annihilation is certainly the only "cure" for him, the viewer, or society more broadly.

## The Reveal That Conceals: Excusing Improper Desire in *Orphan*

Not too long after her adoption by John and Kate Coleman, the otherwise dainty and well-mannered Esther demonstrates a number of increasingly disquieting behaviors: with sadistic indifference, she squashes a pigeon accidentally maimed by the couple's teenaged son (whom she later threatens to castrate); she breaks a schoolmate's leg; and she cracks her own arm in a vice to fabricate evidence of domestic abuse. Perhaps the most troubling and potentially destructive expression of her villainy, however, concerns her transgression of sexual boundaries, especially her attempt to seduce John, whose relationship with his wife she has successfully derailed. Whereas in *Hard Candy* the child functions as a disguised expression of adult authority, in *Orphan* the child is finally revealed as (spoiler alert) an *actual* adult, subject to a rare proportional dwarfism that enables her (with a little makeup) to masquerade as a nine-year-old girl. I have previously suggested that the child villain's horror frequently lies in his or her uncanny confusion of categories: again and again in films like *The Bad Seed* (1956), *Village of the Damned* (1960), and *Joshua* (2007), we see the child's monstrousness as symptomatic of his or her encroachment on the different domain of the adult. The revelation of Esther's origin and nature clearly revillainizes her through her uncanny confusion of adult and child. However, this confusion works more conservatively to assuage the anxieties over pedophilia in which she has been worryingly embroiled.

In *The Omen* (1976), the expectation that the child will provide a narcissistic reflection of his (male) parent can be inferred through

Antichrist brat Damien's refusal to play this role. In his desire for and investment in his son, Robert Thorn requests the child to perform as a facsimile of himself, one that cutely naturalizes the power he has attained. Instead, *The Omen* offers us a parodic inversion of the child's reflection of the status quo. While bearing all the telltale signs of bourgeois male capitalist power, Damien rudely heralds its apocalyptic downfall. In *Orphan*, the child as a narcissistic reflection of its parents is similarly evoked, although disguised through the apparent altruism of adoption. Kate and John Coleman's adoption of Esther is tenderly prefigured by the stillbirth of a baby girl. Kate has a garden shrine to "Jessica" and voices her desire to transfer the love she felt for the lost child to a child in need. This apparently tender motivation for adoption obscures and romanticizes the couple's focus on the child as a construction, a wonderful projection of their hopes and wishes. Given that the mourned child she is set to replace exists as an almost total abstraction, without history or agency, Esther (a real child with both) is surrounded by anxiety because of her ability to contradict that projection. This obsession with the perfect child is foregrounded by the couple's amply illustrated lack of interest in their existing children, a teenaged boy and deaf girl of five or six. Kate's occupation as a composer is placed in firm opposition to her daughter's hearing impairment: early in the film, the daughter (oblivious to her own noisy ineptitude) repeatedly hurls a basketball against the wall behind which Kate is painstakingly composing a downtempo piece. This girl is not enough like her mother. Thus, the twist that Esther is a disguised adult (and one not far removed in age from Kate herself) exposes the obscene reality of Kate's narcissism. This child is much more—too much more—like Kate than she realizes. Late in the film, the subtext weighs in rather heavily when the undisguised Esther accuses Kate of "taking her family for granted," thus implying the selfishness of her motives for adoption. Particularly given the film's surfeit of product placement, *Orphan* uncomfortably exposes children's resemblance to consumer products in the adult imaginary, products that aid in the construction of one's own desired identity.[2]

Despite *Orphan*'s novel presentation of the child villain as a punitive force, Esther's monstrous Otherness is of course sufficiently reinscribed toward the film's conclusion through her revelation as a disturbed adult. In the final, gradual dissembling of her masquerade—"childlike" makeup smearily removed, scars uncovered—Esther's body is reduced through a series of close-ups to repugnantly decontextualized fragments (the same close-ups that detailed the "freakish" application of cosmetics by transgendered psycho Buffalo Bill [Ted Levine] in Jonathan Demme's *The Silence of the Lambs* [1991]). At this point, and much like *Hard Candy*, the film stabilizes into a familiar formula: Esther becomes a female villain on par with the psycho nanny (Rebecca De Mornay) in *The Hand that Rocks the Cradle* or bunny boiler Glenn Close in *Fatal Attraction* (1987). This stabilization is ideological as well as narrative. First, this means the previously scrutinized and distrusted discourse of parental love can be comfortably resurrected. An idealized parental love is reconfirmed at the film's conclusion through John and Kate's urgent protection of their daughter from the imposter. Most importantly, however, the film has the effect of conveniently defusing the pedophilic anxieties through which Esther has been framed in her attempt to seduce John. According to a psychiatrist who tips off Kate, Esther seeks to seduce the fathers of the families into which she is adopted, killing the entire household upon her failure. In presenting herself as a startlingly sexual object, Esther not only realizes a constant anxiety throughout the film over the exposure of children to sexuality but also evidences a fear of pedophilia so pervasive that anyone might horrifyingly find him- or herself touched and contaminated by its monstrous alterity.

## "Fucking Children"

Prior to Esther's adoption, we see Kate rebuff John's sexual advances, which he accepts with good-humored resignation. His desires are put under considerably more pressure, however, by the arrival of the adopted child, through whom the film plays out the adult frustration with children as irritating stiflers of their parents' sex life, amplifying a regular (and regularly managed) disruption to paranoiac proportion (Esther's interruption of her parents' sex is timed with seemingly clairvoyant efficiency). More than merely fostering our antipathy toward Esther as a cause of sexual frustration, these interruptions evidence a profound fear of the child's contamination by or involvement in adult sexual desire and suggest the ease with which an adult might find himself wooed and subdued, if not merely distracted, by the eroticism of the child.

These preoccupations are first evoked on a stormy night we sense heralds the onset of Esther's delinquency. Standing at the foot of the bed and surveying her already sleeping partner, Kate ducks under the covers and begins pleasuring John from below, her entire body obscured from our view. Meanwhile, Esther, spookily attuned to her parents' energies, sits up in her bed with Draculean poise, her gaze cast offscreen in the direction (confirmed through a further cross-cut) of her new parents' lovemaking. She begins to creep through the house presumably in their direction. Yet the first-person view to which we are treated—which obscures totally its subject—casts doubt on whether it is, in fact, the same problem child who is moving and not perhaps one of the other kids, subtly preparing us for the revelation of an unexpected viewer in the tradition of *Halloween*. With this roving subject's identity and motives concealed, the cross-cut back to John and the hidden Kate anxiously positions the child within the same affective moment, particularly when John peeks beneath the covers as if to confirm the presence of his wife and not someone else. "Hi," he giggles.

However fleetingly, we have been made fully ready to believe that Esther has somehow taken the place of the worryingly hidden Kate, a switch of partners during oral sex familiar from comedies like *Say It Isn't So* (2001) and *Revenge of the Nerds* (1984)—although demonstrated more recently in a horror context in *Black Swan* (2010). It isn't Esther under the covers (she appears menacingly illuminated above her adoptive sister instead), although the scene's cross-cutting, its nervous obscuring of both child and adult bodies, and John's otherwise inane address to his hidden partner provoke fear of the child's worrying closeness to adult sex. John's need to rerecognize his lover suggests that in having "unacceptably" relaxed his parental persona, he might unwittingly become the perpetrator of child abuse (perhaps in echo of Nabokov's *Lolita*, in which Humbert's role as apparently naive and passive receiver of oral sex from his eleven-year-old step-daughter assists in disguising the reality of his adult control). In the world of *Orphan*, pedophilia is so virulent a force that one must not only be ever watchful for child predators but also, more troublingly, be ever watchful of *oneself*, alert to the potential misreading or misdirection of one's own behavior. This reading of the scene is subtly consolidated later in the film through Kate's suspicion of John's fidelity. In light of his flirtation with another woman (a flirtation betrayed by Esther), Kate reconstructs her husband as a never quite reformed adulterer, a man whose mind during sex could, very well, be troublingly "somewhere else."

This test of (especially male) sexual propriety is carried further when Esther, her sister in tow and under the pretext of a fear of lightning, finally does disrupt the couple's lovemaking in the same scene, requesting to sleep in their bed. Esther declares, "I want to sleep next to Daddy," clambering over Kate's body toward John as, beneath the covers, he hurriedly attempts to pull on his pajamas. The scene concludes with a shot of Esther snugly clinging to John's back, having replaced his lover at the moment of sexual excitement—an excitement he must now urgently repress. Later, and following a handful of incidents that work to further evidence her psychopathy (albeit episodes played out largely outside her parents' direct knowledge or gaze), Esther again sabotages her parents' sexual expression. With the kids in bed and despite Kate's hesitation, John daringly launches an encounter in the kitchen, taking his wife from behind. But the couple's passion is dissipated with horrific spontaneity when John looks up to discover Esther standing in an adjoining room, bearing full witness to this primal scene—the couple's heady passion potentially transformed into their new daughter's trauma. Esther's ceaseless and damning evocation of her new parents as sexual beings, and the terror with which these moments are imbued, indicate the film's obsession with parental impression management. John and Kate must remain unwaveringly vigilant in the maintenance of a child-friendly persona for fear of being misconstrued as perverse violators of innocence. John later approaches Esther to gently explain what she saw, and she surprises him with seeming indifference. She already knows that adults "fuck." The couple, however, dismiss this language as a meaningless quirk of their adopted daughter's upbringing, assuming that she remains appropriately unaware of the true nature and nuance of sex. Consequently, the fear that he might damagingly (and criminally) expose the child to adult sexuality is one waiting to face John more confrontingly later in the film.

## "I don't know what to do!": Blurred Vision, Blurred Boundaries

Having thoroughly misdirected and frustrated her adoptive father's sexuality, Esther pushes the film's pedophilic tension to its zenith when she attempts to seduce John in Kate's absence, fully narrowing the focus on parental diligence (or negligence) to male sexuality. Slumped melancholically on the sofa, John smokes as he hastily imbibes nearly the entire contents of a bottle of wine, this signifier of his depression serving to indicate his vulnerability to whatever the scheming Esther is preparing (as cross-cutting assures us) in another room. Despite the knife Esther carries with her, it is a more psychologically slippery type of challenge that she will present. The knife accompanies a cheese platter, a fittingly romantic match for John's wine. "What are you wearing?" John slurs as she moves into his blurred view in her strapless black dress, her features—eyes, lashes, mouth—suddenly wetly dark and embossed through layers of makeup. "Look at you." He shakes his head dizzily as she snuggles next to him on the couch. "What have you done to your face?" "I don't want to be alone, I'm scared," Esther pleads, playing on his duty as protector. "Let me take care of you," she offers before he sits upright and clearly demarcates their relationship: "You are so confused. . . . I don't love you like that; that's the way Kate and I love each other." Esther persists, "I don't think anyone really thinks about what you want," playing to the viewer's knowledge of John's ceaselessly deferred orgasm.

Drunk and devastated, John slips into speaking to her as if she were an adult: "I'm just very tired. I don't know what to do—it's difficult," he sobs, seemingly indifferent or impervious to her fingers running lovingly through his hair. Suddenly he remembers himself and flings Esther's hand from his thigh where, outside the frame, it has wandered with disturbing stealth. In this scene, John's sexuality is under its most persecutory review. The male's sexuality has not merely been frustratingly deferred but—more horrifyingly—prepared for *testing* by pedophilia. The banal demonization of children for their seemingly willful interruption of adult intimacy gives way to the horror that one might, under the right circumstances, slip into pedophilia *almost by accident*.

*Orphan* demonstrates that part of the hostility of Esther's new brother toward his new sister is based on his ongoing Oedipal attachment to his mother, whose affections Esther has easily stolen. Holed up in his hideout with his buddies, he ogles issues of *Hustler*, recommending a centerfold to one of his pals. Yet he is embarrassed to have the apparently exotic object of his gaze identified as much too familiar: "She looks like your mom," the friend announces. While the film fails to develop this Oedipal parallel (the boy exists henceforth only to be coerced and terrorized by his new sister), the acknowledgment of his desire injects into the film the possibility of repressed sexual attraction between parent

Figure 9.3. The (only apparently) nine-year-old Esther (Isabelle Fuhrman) offers to "take care of" her adoptive father (Peter Sarsgaard) in Jaume Collet-Serra's *Orphan* (Dark Castle/Appian Way, 2009). Digital frame enlargement.

and child. While John does not commit any act we could confidently label pedophilic, the film's disturbing blurring of the sexual boundaries between adult and child (especially through Esther's sexualized appearance) is disconcerting enough to require exorcism. Esther's status as an adult, revealed immediately after this encounter, neatly intervenes to save us any worry, comfortably reframing John's narrowly avoided lapse.

Following the psychiatrist's account of Esther's origins and adulthood, the film seems to suggest that her psychopathy stems from her serial refusal by men on account of her dwarfism. Putting aside for a moment that Esther needs to maintain her cover in this particular instance by dressing as a little girl, the viewer wonders why she has (according to the psychiatrist) committed herself to imitating a nine-year-old girl for most of her life, a strategy that (one hopes) can only foster her sexual rejection more. The inattention to this part of the narrative bespeaks the primacy of Esther's role in aggressively testing the propriety of adult sexuality, of acting as a paranoiac expression of the possible closeness of pedophilic desire. Of course, despite the "adulthood" that intervenes to allay these anxieties, the viewer must surely be aware that Esther is ultimately played by a child actress: her depiction as a thirtysomething woman is achieved through the same cosmetic skill that passed her off as a child within the diegesis. By contrast, Ellen Page was seventeen at the time of filming *Hard Candy* and eighteen by the time the public saw it. Thus, *Orphan* is careful not to show more of actress Isabelle Fuhrman than its twist can plausibly "redress." As it stands, Esther's adulthood not only attributes to her sufficient agency to compromise the scene's pedophilic framing, demonizing her as a very knowing seductress, but it finally alleviates the gravity of any desires she may have stirred up.

## Conclusion

In *Hard Candy* and *Orphan*, we see cultural artifacts of the intense anxiety attached to emerging conceptions of the child in the early twenty-first century. Both films raise serious questions about the vehemence of our attachment to the notion of the innocent and fundamentally asexual child and the fear of his or her contamination. More pressingly, though, they rely on the audience's desperation to be exempted from a socially abhorred problem that nevertheless, in both *Hard Candy* and *Orphan*, escapes serious scrutiny or analysis. *Hard Candy*'s vigilante child provides a unique instance of the predatory child in the horror genre going to work for adult viewers, assuring them of their own identity and forcefully making sure they know exactly who they are not. Jeff's sudden reinscription of his own villainy clearly quarantines him from us, rescuing us from our failure to recognize his Otherness and our implication in his voyeuristic gaze. In *Orphan*, the solution to pedophilia and the accusations of sexual contamination to which Esther's parents have been increasingly subject is to remove the child from the equation altogether. Both films demonstrate a deeply threatening awareness of child sexual abuse. Both are also finally overpowered by their anxieties, reducing them to formulaic and familiar conflicts so that, at best, they present only stunning negations of the insecurities they raise.

# Afterword

In popular cinema as well as popular culture, the symbolic space of the child has been thoroughly colonized. The horror film's little monsters paint a remarkable picture of adults' reliance on fictional definitions of the child imbued with often ludicrous, even mystical, expectations. Through their chaotic disruption in horror, we can see children as mystified representatives of class difference and their role in naturalizing systems of oppression; we can see them as a reflection of the morality, social status, and reproductive caliber of their parents. Ideas of children as innocent and vulnerable are powerfully invoked through the way adults are accustomed to looking them, thus registering with paranoiac terror the idea of a truly active, looking child. In *The Exorcist*, we can see the image of the innocent child played out as a figure in a spiritual battle, forever in conflict with independent adulthood.

Despite having a heyday in the 1970s, the child villain remains a forceful and enduring figure in the horror film well into the 2000s. When Kathy Merlock Jackson observed a decline in the "child-as-monster-film" in the mid-1980s, she attributed this to the effect of the child villain having "hinged on shock value" (152); depictions of children that conflict with their traditional image as innocent tend to "stabilize as cultures learn to cope with them" (154). In hindsight, we can see that monstrous children have never left: our ability to "get used" to this figure is hindered by the ever-increasing vehemence of dominant ideological assumptions surrounding childhood. The recent resurgence in child protection rhetoric as a response to the horror of pedophilia has had the effect of recharging the child as a symbol of innocence and vulnerability—a development sensationally capitalized on by *Hard Candy* (2005) and *Orphan* (2009). And as those films, along with *The Omen* (2006), *Joshua* (2007), and *The Unborn* (2009), indicate, the child villain shows little sign of abating.

In the moody drama *We Need to Talk About Kevin* (2011), the child villain of horror is given a surprisingly straightforward legitimization. From his emergence as an incessantly shrieking infant, Kevin terrorizes his mother (Tilda Swinton), a vision of raw-eyed and tense-mouthed maternal anguish. The child's psychopathy is clearly depicted at various stages of his development. As a baby, Kevin will cunningly curtail his infernal shriek for his dad's benefit, just to torment mom that little bit more. By the time the sixteen-year-old Kevin (Ezra Miller) slaughters his classmates in a Columbine-style massacre, we are utterly positive that his delinquency is innate and irreparable. There is scarcely an instant of *We Need to Talk about Kevin* that does not serve to perturb, harrow, traumatize, discomfort, or generally afflict the viewer in some way, a disorientating, fragmentary style and abundance of tremulous close-ups presenting the film as an aesthetic and thus emotional challenge. Yet this ostensibly "new" aesthetic challenge belies the way in which the film actually restates well-worn clichés of child villainy. Like the child villains of *Orphan* or *The Good Son* (1993), Kevin has an adorable younger sibling who exists to torture the viewer with her vulnerability. And like the brat in *Orphan*, Kevin stymies his parents' sex and overhears everything he shouldn't. Most obviously, the child villain here is essentially (if not literally) demonic. His psychology and villainy are thoroughly unaffected by social or familial context, nor are they ever genuinely addressed beyond their horrific effects. We might note that despite Kevin's increasingly alarming behavior (he forces his sister's pet guinea pigs down the garbage disposal, then cunningly orchestrates the girl being mutilated with the drain cleaner used to clear the blockage), psychiatric discourse makes no appearance in the world of the film. In a case like this, we already know there's nothing to be done.

It is clear that adults have not consciously orchestrated the traditional images of the child that are so prone to subversion in horror. Dominant understandings of the child are scarcely thought of as symbolic fictions; they are "the child's natural reality," ideological perspectives that overlay real children with constructed images. As Joann Conrad writes, "The modern construction of childhood as separate from adulthood, and as a protected, privileged place of innocence, is a by now naturalized phenomenon" (185). Inconveniently for the adult, though, this ideological lens is too rose-tinted for us to truly believe what we see through it. As long as our cultural contemplation of childhood remains caught in a gauzy fantasy of untainted innocence, those implausible visions will inevitably be subject to doubt. Not only do child villains demonstrate the romanticized meanings children sustain for adults, but they also come as stunning evidence of the unmanageable constriction of those meanings.

Just as the child villain owes his or her effect to our attachment to an ideal child, cultural responses to child criminality often subject very real children to our misperceptions. On the 1993 abduction and murder of toddler James Bulger by ten-year-old boys in England, Allison James and Chris Jenks write that "the murder was not just disturbing, but was, quite literally, unthinkable. Unthinkable, that is, because it occurred within the conceptual space of childhood which, prior to this breach, was conceived of—for the most part and for most children—as innocence enshrined" (1). Addressing child criminality in the media, Stewart Asquith points out that the Bulger killing was surrounded by a feeling of the "killing of innocence" (167). Such a challenge, far from leading to sober review of the constructed nature of childhood, produces the construction of Joann Conrad's "Janus-faced, good/evil child" (185) through which "evil" is quarantined to a figure of its own where it cannot infect the idea of the innocent child. Thus, in Merlock Jackson's terms, images of the terrible child may indeed have begun to stabilize, although it is hardly a desirable stabilization. Nor is this stabilization, in fact, very stable. As Conrad points out, "[a]s the two visions of the child become more and more essentialized and mutually exclusive, the tension between them increases" (185). The increasingly dichotomized figure of the child in the public sphere serves only to perpetuate the fraught myth of emblematic innocence.

The horror film confirms and complements with grim force the "evil child," even going so far as to imply its basis in "incontrovertible" biblical scripture. Whereas the more influential of the 1950s teen rebellion films, like *The Wild One* (1953) and *Rebel Without a Cause* (1955), urged improved relations between children and their parents, situating juvenile delinquency as part of broader social malfunction, the child villain in horror has consistently reinforced the division between adults and children, suppressing the ideological construction of children and exploiting it in the name of terror.

It takes little imagination to believe that fictional definitions of the child intersect with and influence public attitudes to real children. For Marina Warner, the myth of childhood as a distinct, rarefied condition of innocence "is not fallacious, or merely repressive—myths are not only delusions—chimaeras"; we must recognize that it "also tell[s] stories which can give shape and substance to practical, social measures" (46–47). The social force of the representations of children in horror demands extensive investigation because of the ability of the genre's clichés to infiltrate journalistic discourse on childhood criminality (as commentators such as Julian Petley and Salman Rushdie have observed). When child crime ruptures our innocent definitions of children, urging our reconsideration of the way power and socialization are conducted in intergenerational terms, the divisive caricatures of the horror film are a suggestive presence. Similarly, although on a more pedestrian scale, we might suggest that the representations of horror serve to aesthetically contain and demonize justifiable child anger or disobedience. Joseph Zornado has argued that what is culturally and unquestioningly termed "misbehavior" in children "is an adult description of what is more accurately perfect behavior given the conditions of the child's existence" (206). In horror film, we find a handy yet even more powerful and aggressive conceptual vocabulary.

Of course, given the horror film's adult-exclusive nature, it is not a legitimate domain in which real children can resist the definitions projected on to them by adults. The child villain is firmly rooted in what the adult desires of the child, not the expression of children's desires for themselves. The monstrous doll of *Child's Play* (1988) undoubtedly finds reference in children's real-world interest in consumer products and the pressure parents feel to purchase these. However, the film's hellish vision of those consumer desires is a distinctly adult fantasy, the child's need for stimulation and excitement reprocessed into a nightmare of insatiability and financial persecution. It is also through this process of reimagination and reinscription that behaviors through which children *might* attempt to "speak"—to define themselves outside of adult parameters—are sensitively intuited and aggressively denigrated. Claudia Mitchell and Jacqueline Reid-Walsh have investigated the logic of children's play, the representational qualities of their consumer products, and the emotional landscape in which the child situates them. Yet through the specifically adult lens of the horror film, children's toys occur as offensive declarations of division, superstitious totems that endanger the adult's control. Similarly, the idea of the child "looking" from a place of subjective independence is explosively maligned, translated into fantasies of voyeurism, violence, and hypnotic control.

Reviewing our cultural treatment of and attitudes toward children necessitates profound consideration of popular film as a dominant artistic medium in contemporary Western culture and serious attention to its capacity to influence public perceptions. In this respect, the horror film remains a telling and urgent domain for analysis of adult/child relations and attitudes. The history of child horror cinema is capable of revealing to us the sheer breadth, volatility, and absurdity of the fictionalization of childhood and putting light on the destructive and paranoid representations to which it gives birth.

# Notes

## Introduction

1. For a discussion of constructions of childhood with which Rousseau's competed and eventually supplanted (such as those focused on original sin), see Cunningham 41–80.

2. For more on the adult political desires embedded in this recharged conceptualization of the child, see Spigel 112.

3. In the documentary *Something To Do with Death* (2003), Leone biographer Christopher Frayling points out that the notion of archetypal cinema good guy and idealist Fonda shooting a child was considered so disturbing that the scene was frequently censored for American television.

## Chapter 2

1. Patty McCormack went on to star in the low-budget thrillers *Mommy* (1995), and its sequel *Mommy's Day* (1997), two films about a murderous, wealthy single mother and almost certainly intended as unofficial sequels to *The Bad Seed*. In *Mommy's* opening scene, McCormack kills her daughter's teacher because the little girl narrowly misses out on a class award to an underprivileged Mexican student.

## Chapter 3

1. Steve Neale discusses the manner in which "threat and aggression are a function both of [the now grown-up villain's] point of view and of the limits on our vision as spectators provided by the articulation of the frame" (362).

2. For instance, according to Lacan, the male voyeur is trying to see "the object as absence . . . merely a shadow, a shadow behind the curtain. . . . What he is looking for is not . . . the phallus—but precisely its absence" (182).

# Chapter 6

1. John Moore's 2006 remake of *The Omen* cheekily integrates itself with *Rosemary's Baby* through the stunt casting of Mia Farrow as Mrs. Baylock, Damien's nanny protector.

# Chapter 7

1. Seeking to tap into the enormous success of religious thriller *The Exorcist* (1973), *The Omen* used the name of the earlier film's protagonist for its villain.

2. For a rundown of *The Exorcist*'s sensational reception, see William Paul 288.

# Chapter 9

1. In the film's DVD commentary, the filmmakers briefly mention that Clint Eastwood's spaghetti-influenced *High Plains Drifter* (1973), a dreamlike Western in which the unnamed out-of-towner exacts revenge on a band of outlaws who murdered the town sheriff years earlier, was one of many films they were thinking about during the shooting of the scene. Hayley's red hoodie in *Hard Candy* provides a possible connection to that film, in which the town, painted entirely red and renamed "Hell," becomes a bizarre theater of divine retribution.

2. Helmut Wintersberger has suggested that the twentieth and early twenty-first century sentimentalization of childhood has placed children within the category of consumer durables: "Children are neither born as assets for their parents' old-age security nor for their own sake, but for the sake of their parents' self-realization" (204). *Orphan*'s tagline very efficiently relied on the conceptualization of the child as the ultimate, potentially faulty (and unreturnable!) consumer product: "There's something wrong with Esther." While not offering us the slightest intimation of what is wrong with Esther, the line powerfully indicates that even the tiniest compromise to this idealized product is enough. One might say that in her villainy, Esther threateningly demystifies the ideological lens of her new parents' love, revealing that love as the gauzy packaging of the sordidly self-centered in that adoption is a form of "purchase" or "acquisition."

# Works Cited

Ariès, Philippe. *Centuries of Childhood: A Social History of Family Life*. New York: Jonathan Cape, 1962.

Asquith, Stewart. "When Children Kill Children: The Search for Justice." Jenks 164–81.

Baudrillard, Jean. *Selected Writings*. Cambridge: Polity, 1988.

Beard, William. "The Visceral Mind: The Major Films of David Cronenberg." *The Shape of Rage: The Films of David Cronenberg*. Ed. Piers Handling. New York: Zoetrope, 1983. 1–79.

Best, Joel, and Gerald T. Horiuchi. "The Razor Blade in the Apple: The Social Construction of Urban Legends." *Social Problems* 32.5 (1985): 488–99.

Blake, William. "The Mental Traveller." *The Complete Poems*. Ed. Alicia Ostriker. London: Penguin, 1978. 499.

Blatty, William Peter. *The Exorcist*. London: Corgi, 1971.

Bocock, Robert. *Consumption*. London: Routledge, 1993.

Brunvand, Jan Harold. *The Vanishing Hitchhiker*. New York: Norton, 1981.

Büssing, Sabine. *Aliens in the Home: The Child in Horror Fiction*. Oxford: Greenwood, 1987.

Carroll, Noël. *The Philosophy of Horror: Or, Paradoxes of the Heart*. London: Routledge, 1990.

Cavan, Ruth Shonle, and Theodore N. Ferdinand. *Juvenile Delinquency*. 3rd ed. Philadelphia: J. B. Lippincott, 1975.

Clover, Carol J. "Her Body, Himself: Gender in the Slasher Film." *Representations* 20 (1987): 187–228.

"Comic Books and Juvenile Delinquency." Interim Report on the Committee on the Judiciary Pursuant to S. Res. 89 and S. Res. 190. 1955–6 <http://www.thecomicbooks.com/1955senateinterim.html>.

Conrad, Joann. "Lost Innocent and Sacrificial Delegate: The JonBenet Ramsey Murder." Jenks 182–222.

Coveney, Peter. *The Image of Childhood*. London: Penguin, 1967.

Coyne, John. *The Piercing*. 1978. Neocon Books, 2010.

Creed, Barbara. *The Monstrous-Feminine: Film, Feminism, Psychoanalysis*. New York: Routledge, 1993.

Cross, Gary. *The Cute and the Cool: Wondrous Innocence and Modern American Children's Culture*. New York: Oxford UP, 2004.

Cunningham, Hugh. *Children and Childhood in Western Society Since 1500*. Harlow, UK: Pearson, 2005.

Davis-Floyd, Robbie and Joseph Dumit. "Cyborg Babies: Children of the Third Millennium." *Cyborg Babies: From Techno-Sex to Techno-Tots*. Ed. Robbie Davis-Floyd and Joseph Dumit. New York: Routledge, 1998. 1–18.

De Felitta, Frank. *Audrey Rose*. New York: Warner Books, 1975.

Derry, Charles. *Dark Dreams 2.0: A Psychological History of the Modern Horror Film from the 1950s to the 21st Century*. Jefferson, NC: McFarland, 2009.

Ebert, Roger. Rev. of *Hard Candy*, dir. David Slade. *RogerEbert.com* 28 Apr. 2006. 20 Aug. 2011 <http://rogerebert.suntimes.com/apps/pbcs.dll/article?AID=/20060427/REVIEWS/60421003>.

Freud, Sigmund. "On Narcissism: An Introduction." *Collected Papers*. Ed. John D. Sutherland. Vol. IV. London: Hogarth, 1957. 30–59.

———. "The Uncanny." *The Standard Edition of the Complete Psychological Works of Sigmund Freud*. Ed. James Strachey. Vol. XVII. London: Hogarth, 1955. 219–56.

Gilbert, James. *A Cycle of Outrage: America's Reaction to the Juvenile Delinquent in the 1950s*. New York: Oxford UP, 1986.

Goffman, Erving. *The Presentation of Self in Everyday Life*. London: Allen Lane/ The Penguin Press, 1969.

Goldberg, Ruth. "Demons in the Family: Tracking the Japanese 'Uncanny Mother Film' from *A Page of Madness* to *Ringu*." Grant and Sharrett 370–85.

Golub, Adam. "They Turned a School into a Jungle!: How *The Blackboard Jungle* Redefined the Education Crisis in Postwar America." *Film and History: An Interdisciplinary Journal of Film and Television Studies* 39.1 (2009): 21–30.

Grant, Barry Keith, and Christopher Sharrett, eds. *Planks of Reason: Essays on the Horror Film*. Lanham, MD: Scarecrow, 2004.

Grant, Barry Keith. "Rich and Strange: The Yuppie Horror Film." Grant and Sharrett 153–69.

Green, David A. "Suitable Vehicles: Framing Blame and Justice When Children Kill a Child." *Crime Media Culture* 4.2 (2008). 197–220.

Hendershot, Cyndy. "The Cold War Horror Film: Taboo and Transgression in *The Bad Seed*, *The Fly*, and *Psycho*." *Journal of Popular Film and Television* 29.1 (2001): 21–39.

Hoffmann, E. T. A. "The Sandman" ("Der Sandmann"). *Tales of Hoffmann*. 1816. Penguin, 1982. 85–126.

Hoppenstand, Gary. "Exorcising the Devil Babies: Images of Children and Adolescents in the Best-Selling Horror Novel." *Images of the Child*. Ed. Harry Eiss. Bowling Green, OH: Popular, 1994. 35–58.

Hutchings, Peter. *The Horror Film*. Harlow, Eng.: Pearson Longman, 2004.

Irigaray, Luce. "Women-mothers, The Silent Substratum of the Social Order." *The Irigaray Reader*. Trans. David Macey. Ed. Margaret Whitford. Oxford: Blackwell, 1991. 47–52.

Jackson, Chuck. "Little, Violent, White: *The Bad Seed* and the Matter of Children." *Journal of Popular Film and Television* 28.2 (2000): 64–78.

James, Allison, and Chris Jenks. "Public Perceptions of Childhood Criminality." Jenks 127–43.

James, Henry. *The Turn of the Screw.* 1898. Clinton, MA: Airmont, 1967.

Jenkins, Henry, ed. *The Children's Culture Reader.* New York: New York UP, 1998.

Jenks, Chris, ed. *Childhood: Critical Concepts in Sociology.* Vol. 3. New York: Routledge, 2005.

Kaplan, E. Ann. *Women and Film: Both Sides of the Camera.* London: Routledge, 1983.

———. "Sex, Work and Motherhood: The Impossible Triangle." *The Journal of Sex Research* 27.3 (1990): 409–25.

Kenway, Jane, and Elizabeth Bullen. "Inventing the Young Consumer." *Childhood: Critical Concepts in Sociology.* Ed. Chris Jenks. Vol. 2. London: Routledge, 2005. 199–228.

Kermode, Mark. Rev. of *Hard Candy*, dir. David Slade. *The Guardian.* 18 June 2006. 17 Mar. 2014 <http://www.theguardian.com/film/2006/jun/18/features.review>.

Kermode, Mark. *BFI Modern Classics: The Exorcist.* 2nd ed. 1998. London: Palgrave Macmillan, 2003.

Kincaid, James R. *Child-Loving: The Erotic Child in Victorian Culture.* New York: Routledge, 1992.

———. "Producing Erotic Children." Jenkins 241–52.

Kincheloe, Joe L. "The New Childhood: Home Alone As a Way of Life." Jenkins 159–77.

Kristeva, Julia. "The Adolescent Novel." *Abjection, Melancholia, and Love: The Work of Julia Kristeva.* Ed. John Fletcher and Andrew Benjamin. London: Routledge, 1989. 8–23.

Krzywinska, Tanya. "Demon Daddies: Gender, Ecstasy and Terror in the Possession Film." *Horror Film Reader.* Ed. Alain Silver and James Ursini. New York: Limelight, 2000. 247–67.

Kuhn, Reinhard. *Corruption in Paradise: The Child in Western Literature.* Hanover: Brown UP, 1982.

Lacan, Jacques. *The Four Fundamental Concepts of Psycho-analysis.* Trans. Alain Sheridan. Ed. Jacques-Alain Miller. London: Hogarth, 1977.

Leclaire, Serge. *A Child Is Being Killed: On Primary Narcissism and the Death Drive.* 1975. Trans. Marie-Claude Hays. Stanford: Stanford UP, 1998.

Lewis, John. "'Mother Oh God Mother' . . .": Analysing the 'Horror' of Single Mothers in Contemporary Hollywood Horror." *Scope* 2 (2005). 30 Jan. 2009 <http://www.scope.nottingham.ac.uk/article.php?issue=2&id=68>.

March, William. *The Bad Seed.* 1954. Hopewell, NJ: Ecco, 1997.

Masschelein, Anneleen. "A Homeless Concept: Shapes of the Uncanny in Twentieth-Century Theory and Culture." *Image and Narrative* 5 (2003). 31 Jan. 2008 <http://www.imageandnarrative.be/inarchive/uncanny/anneleen-masschelein.htm>.

Matthews, Gareth B. *Philosophy and the Young Child*. Cambridge, MA: Harvard UP, 1980.

McDonagh, Maitland. *Broken Mirrors/Broken Minds: The Dark Dreams of Dario Argento*. London: Sun Tavern Fields, 1994.

Mead, Margaret. "Halloween, Where Has All the Mischief Gone?" *Aspects of the Present*. New York: William Morrow, 1980. 201–7.

Medovoi, Leerom. *Youth and the Cold War Origins of Identity*. Durham: Duke UP, 2005.

Merish, Lori. "Cuteness and Commodity Aesthetics: Tom Thumb and Shirley Temple." *Freakery: Cultural Spectacles of the Extraordinary Body*. Ed. Rosemarie Garland-Thomson. New York: New York UP, 1996. 185–203.

Merlock Jackson, Kathy. *Images of Children in American Film*. Metuchen, NJ: Scarecrow, 1986.

Mitchell, Claudia, and Jacqueline Reid-Walsh. *Researching Children's Popular Culture: The Cultural Spaces of Childhood*. London: Routledge, 2002.

Moore, Lisa Jean. *Sperm Counts: Overcome by Man's Most Precious Fluid*. New York: New York UP, 2007.

———, and Heidi Durkin. "The Leaky Male Body: Forensics and the Construction of the Sexual Subject." *Medicalized Masculinities*. Ed. Dana Rosenfeld and Christopher A. Faircloth. Philadelphia: Temple UP, 2006. 65–88.

Mulvey, Laura. "Visual Pleasure and Narrative Cinema." *Screen* 16.3 (1975): 6–28.

Muncie, John. *Youth and Crime: A Critical Introduction*. London: Sage, 1999.

Nabokov, Vladimir. *Lolita*. 1955. New York: Vintage, 1997.

Neale, Steve. "*Halloween*: Suspense, Aggression and the Look." Grant and Sharrett 356–69.

Pattison, Robert. *The Child Figure in English Literature*. Athens: U of Georgia P, 1978.

Paul, William. *Laughing Screaming: Modern Hollywood Horror and Comedy*. New York: Columbia UP, 1994.

Petchesky, Rosalind Pollack. "Fetal Images: The Power of Visual Culture in the Politics of Reproduction." *Feminist Studies* 13.2 (1987): 263–92.

Petley, Julian. "The Monstrous Child." *The Body's Perilous Pleasures: Dangerous Desires and Contemporary Culture*. Ed. Michele Aaron. Wiltshire: Edinburgh UP, 1999. 87–107.

Pisters, Patricia. *The Matrix of Visual Culture: Working with Deleuze in Film Theory*. Stanford, CA: Stanford UP, 2003.

Pomerance, Murray. *The Horse Who Drank the Sky: Film Experience beyond Narrative and Theory*. New Brunswick, NJ: Rutgers UP, 2008.

Postman, Neil. *The Disappearance of Childhood*. London: W. H. Allen, 1982.

Qvortrup, Jens. "Varieties of Childhood." *Studies in Modern Childhood: Society, Agency, Culture*. Ed. Jens Qvortrup. New York: Palgrave Macmillan, 2005. 1–20.

Rogin, Michael. "Kiss Me Deadly: Communism, Motherhood, and Cold War Movies." *Representations* 6 (1984): 1–36.

Rothman, Barbara Katz. *The Tentative Pregnancy: Prenatal Diagnosis and the Future of Motherhood*. New York: Viking Press, 1986.

Rousseau, Jean-Jacques. *Émile*. 1762. London: Dent, 1974.

Rushdie, Salman. "The Release of the Bulger Killers." *Step across This Line*. London: Jonathon Cape, 2002. 381–83.

Rutherford, Jonathan. *Men's Silences: Predicaments in Masculinity*. London: Routledge, 1992.

Sandford, Christopher. *McQueen: The Biography*. London: HarperCollins, 2001.

Scheib, Richard. Rev. of *The Brood*, dir. David Cronenberg. *Moria: Science Fiction, Horror and Fantasy Film Review* 18 Sep. 2008. 17 Mar. 2014 <http://moria.co.nz/horror/brood-1979.htm>.

Schor, Juliet B. *Born to Buy: The Commercialized Child and the New Consumer Culture*. New York: Scribner, 2004.

Scott, Lindsey. "A Mother's Curse: Reassigning Blame in Hideo Nakata's *Ringu* and Gore Verbinski's *The Ring*." *Cinephile* 6.2 (2010): 14–19.

Shary, Timothy. *Teen Movies: American Youth On Screen*. London: Wallflower, 2006.

Smith, Murray. *Engaging Characters: Fiction, Emotion and the Cinema*. Oxford: Clarendon Press, 1995.

Spark, Richard F. *The Infertile Male: The Clinician's Guide to Diagnosis and Treatment*. Dordrecht: Kluwer, 1988.

Spigel, Lynn. "Seducing the Innocent: Childhood and Television in Postwar America." Jenkins 110–33.

*Statistics Canada: Canada's National Statistics Agency*. 2 Nov. 2008 <http://www.statcan.gc.ca/start-debut-eng.html/>.

Tatar, Maria. "What Do Children Want?" *American Literary History* 7.4 (1995): 740–49.

"Teen Killer Speaks Out 16 Years Later." *WIVB.com*. 4 Sep. 2012 <http://www.wivb.com/dpp/news/crime/Shocking-teen-killer-speaks-out>.

Valerius, Karyn. "*Rosemary's Baby*, Gothic Pregnancy, and Fetal Subjects." *College Literature* 32.5 (2005): 116–35.

Wallace, William Ross. "The Hand That Rocks The Cradle." 1865. *Magill's Quotations in Context*. Ed. Frank Northen Magill and Tench Francis Tilghman. New York: Harper & Row, 1965. 335.

Warner, Marina. *Six Myths of Our Time*. New York: Vintage, 1994.

"We Will Bury You!" *Time* 27 Nov. 1956. *Time.com*. 13 Nov. 2008 <http://www.time.com/time/magazine/article/0,9171,867329,00.html>.

Wertham, Fredric. *Seduction of the Innocent*. London: Museum Press, 1955.

White, Eric. "Case Study: Nakata Hideo's *Ringu* and *Ringu 2*." *Japanese Horror Cinema*. Ed. Jay McRoy. Edinburgh: Edinburgh UP, 2005. 38–47.

Wintersberger, Helmut. "Work, Welfare and Generational Order: Towards a Political Economy of Childhood." *Studies in Modern Childhood: Society, Agency, Culture*. Ed. Jens Qvortrup. New York: Palgrave Macmillan, 2005. 201–20.

Wood, Robin. "An Introduction to the American Horror Film." Grant and Sharrett 107–41.

Woodson, Stephani Etheridge. "Mapping the Cultural Geography of Childhood or, Performing Monstrous Children." *Journal of American Culture* 22.4 (1999): 31–43.

Woodward, Steven. "She's Murder: Pretty Poisons and Bad Seeds." *Sugar, Spice, and Everything Nice: Cinemas of Girlhood*. Ed. Frances Gateward and Murray Pomerance. Detroit: Wayne State UP, 2002. 303–321.

Worland, Rick. *The Horror Film: An Introduction*. Malden, MA: Blackwell, 2007.

Wylie, Philip. *A Generation of Vipers*. 1942. New York: Rinehart, 1955.

Wyndham, John. *The Midwich Cuckoos*. Aylesbury, Bucks: Penguin, 1957.

Zelizer, Viviana A. *Pricing the Priceless Child: The Changing Social Value of Children*. New York: Basic, 1985.

Zornado, Joseph. *Inventing the Child: Culture, Ideology, and the Story of Childhood*. New York: Garland, 2000.

# Index

Page numbers that appear in italics refer to image captions.